PRAISE FOR WRITING FOR THE SOUL

"Few can write about writing like Jerry Jenkins. Even fewer can do better urging us to write for the soul. He has done so for decades. Any person interested in the high privilege of writing for the soul will delight in and profit from reading this valued work."

> —Max Lucado, bestselling author and senior minister at the Oak Hills Church

"Have you ever wanted to sit with a famous, successful author for hours on end and pick his brain, get advice, drink in his sagely wisdom and experience? Well, now you can. Reading Jerry's book is like sitting and having coffee with him. Here, in a friendly, informal style, are answers, insights, anecdotes and challenges from a guy who has been there and knows. I loved it!"

> —Frank Peretti, bestselling author and novelist

"*Writing for the Soul* is a generous gift from one of the most successful writers of our time. This look into the mind, heart, and soul of a consummate professional will absolutely inspire, instruct, and guide you on your own writing journey. Don't fail to add this one to your bookshelf."

> —James Scott Bell, best-selling novelist and author of *Write Great Fiction: Plot & Structure*

"I've read numerous books written by Jerry B. Jenkins. He's good. I've heard many talks about the craft of writing presented by Jerry B. Jenkins. He's good at that, too. Now, I've read a book about writing by Jerry B. Jenkins. It's the combination of both good options. It's all here: the discipline, the craftsmanship, and the marketing aspects of professional writing; and it's told in story fashion. Enjoy, and learn!"

> —Dr. Dennis E. Hensley, author of *How to Write What You Love and Make a Living at It*

"Jerry Jenkins is perhaps the ultimate authority on writing for the soul! A careful, easy-to-follow look at every aspect of the Christian story-telling process. A must-read for anyone wanting to write the deeper story."

    —Karen Kingsbury, bestselling author of the Redemption Series and *Even Now*

"In *Writing for the Soul*, Jerry Jenkins offers a wealth of information gained through experience and education. New and veteran writers will benefit from reading this collection of philosophies and practical pointers from one of the most successful and down to earth writers of our time."

    —Angela Hunt, bestselling author of *The Novelist*

ALSO BY JERRY B. JENKINS

WRITING FOR THE SOUL

WRITING FOR THE SOUL

Instruction and Advice
from an Extraordinary Writing Life

JERRY B. JENKINS

Author of the Left Behind Series

Foreword by Francine Rivers

WRITER'S DIGEST BOOKS

writersdigestbooks.com
Cincinnati, Ohio

10 09 08 07 06   6 5 4 3 2 1

Distributed in Canada by Fraser Direct
100 Armstrong Avenue
Georgetown, ON, Canada L7G 5S4
Tel: (905) 877-4411

Distributed in the U.K. and Europe by David & Charles
Brunel House, Newton Abbot, Devon, TQ12 4PU, England
Tel: (+44) 1626 323200, Fax: (+44) 1626 323319
E-mail: postmaster@davidandcharles.co.uk

Distributed in Australia by Capricorn Link
P.O. Box 704, Windsor, NSW 2756 Australia
Tel: (02) 4577-3555

Library of Congress Cataloging-in-Publication Data
Jenkins, Jerry B.
   Writing for the soul : instruction and advice from an extraordinary writing life / by Jerry B. Jenkins.--1st ed.
        p. cm.
   Includes index.
   ISBN-13: 978-1-58297-417-0
   ISBN-10: 1-58297-417-9 (alk. paper)
   1. Authorship--Vocational guidance. I. Title.
PN151.J45 2006
808'.02023--dc22
                              2006007566

Editor: Jane Friedman
Designer: Claudean Wheeler
Cover Photograph: Ann Cutting
Production Coordinator: Robin Richie

TO MY WRITING MENTORS

Bonita Jenkins

Richard Carey

Henry Roepken

Linda Hamilton

Stanley Baldwin

Roy Carlisle

and Sol Stein

ACKNOWLEDGMENTS

Thanks to Debra Petkus-Perry
for suggesting this project,
for handling the initial interviewing
and shaping the direction,
and for serving as editorial coordinator.
To John Perrodin
for help in finalizing the manuscript.
And to Jane Friedman
of Writer's Digest Books
for the best experience with an editor
in a lifetime of writing.

Table of Contents

FOREWORD

I met Jerry Jenkins shortly after I signed with Tyndale House Publishers, and the Left Behind phenomenon had not yet happened. Jerry was gracious and encouraging. Over the years, the astounding success of the Left Behind series has not changed him adversely in any way I can see. Admirably, Jerry has risen to the great responsibility his blessings carry, and he has tirelessly encouraged new writers to raise the standard and spread the Gospel through the art of writing. We know it is one thing to be a Christian who writes, and quite another to be a Christian writer. Though this book offers advice and encouragement to both, the heartbeat is to a higher calling, one that will open hearts and minds to a relationship with Jesus and the quest for excellence that will bring praise to our Lord and Savior.

The writing life offers challenges beyond merely learning the craft. Writing for the Lord adds complexities to those challenges. All too often, Christians are seduced by working for the Lord, setting aside the more important relationship with Him in their pursuit to serve Him. What I find most inspiring about Jerry Jenkins's *Writing for the Soul* is his determination and success in keeping his priorities. Love and serve the Lord, and remember He has given you a family to love and serve as well. Jerry made a decision early in his career to put family ahead of writing projects. By the sheer number of newspaper and magazine articles, biographies, nonfiction, and fiction books he has written, I believe the Lord has honored Jerry for that choice, and multiplied his energies.

With his easy flowing, conversational style, always laced with his signature good humor, Jerry shares knowledge gained through a lifetime of hard work writing everything from columns to best-selling novels, many of which have been translated into numerous languages and have sold many millions of copies. His stories have changed lives and hearts around the world. He shares his struggles openly, and by his humble example, inspires us with what the Lord has done through him. He entertains us with anecdotes about the people he has met, often American icons who prove to be as human as the rest of us.

You will enjoy reading this book. From the first page, you will be tempted to put your feet up and drink it in with one pleasurable swallow. Don't. Instead, savor it. Keep pen and paper by your side. There are treasures here; sparks to light the fire, and to keep it burning.

Francine Rivers
Author of *Redeeming Love*

INTRODUCTION
BIG DOOR ON A SMALL HINGE

So there I sat, writing away—as I had nearly every day for more than twenty years—when Rick Christian called. He was my agent.

I liked the sound of having an agent and worked it into as many conversations as possible. I had written and published ninety books before even considering an agent, and to my mind I was already living a writer's dream. While mainstream fiction was my love, I'd made a healthy six-figure income largely by writing famous people's stories. These hadn't been ghost jobs. My name had appeared on the covers of biographies and autobiographies of many luminaries. But of course, the average reader doesn't notice the name of a faceless writer, and more than once I was asked if I had read a certain book—when I had written it. I was the most famous author no one had ever heard of. Having an agent and being able to say *My agent this* and *My agent that* should have lent some credibility to my invisible career, but more likely it repulsed even those who loved me.

Well, the cliché is that big doors turn on small hinges, and the small hinge that day was Rick Christian's call. He had no more idea than I did what would come of that short conversation. To the best of my memory, it went like this:

"Have you ever met Tim LaHaye?"

"No," I said. "Familiar with him, of course."

I knew Dr. LaHaye not only as a former pastor and a bestselling nonfiction writer, but also as an outspoken conservative polemic, big on the study of temperaments, sexuality in the Christian marriage, politics, Christian education, and prophecy. In a former life, as editor of an inspirational knockoff of *TV Guide*, I had assigned and published a cover story on Dr. LaHaye and had also used him as a columnist.

"You need to meet him," Rick said. "I represent him, and he has a great novel idea."

Well, doesn't everybody?

The fact was, I wanted to meet Dr. LaHaye. I had a few doubts about anyone's "great" novel idea, but Rick Christian has always had an eye for good stuff, and both he and LaHaye were willing to come my way and meet me at a hotel near O'Hare Field in Chicago—Rick from Colorado, Dr. LaHaye from California.

The idea proved simple, yet profound. Dr. LaHaye had come up with the idea while flying to a prophecy conference, where he was to speak about his view of the end times, based on his largely literal interpretation of the Bible. (He had written nonfiction books on the subject, and they had enjoyed strong sales.) He saw the pilot emerge from the cabin and flirt with a flight attendant, and he noticed that the captain wore a wedding ring and the attendant did not. The kernel of a plot came to Dr. LaHaye in an instant. He wondered, what if the Rapture[1] occurred right then, and a certain percentage of the people aboard that plane simply vanished in an instant, leaving everything material behind? And what if that pilot's wife was a Christian believer who had talked to him about anticipating that very event?

The notion of fictionalizing an account of the Rapture and those left behind was not entirely new. It had been done a few times, and while always fascinating and popular, the results had rarely done justice to the magnitude of the story. While I loved the idea and the scene

---

[1] Rapture is a term commonly used for the biblically prophesied return of Jesus Christ, when true believers are snatched away into Heaven "in the twinkling of an eye."

Dr. LaHaye described for an opener, my fear was that there was a fine line between drama and schlock.

What impressed me most that day, however, was Dr. LaHaye himself. Already in his late sixties, he was trim, taut, and energetic, full of enthusiasm and passion. He wanted to see this story told in novel form, he said, "because fiction is what most people seem to want to read."

I'm neither a theologian nor a scholar, but I am an evangelical who was raised in churches that believed in this future event. "If I were to attempt this," I said, "who would be my target audience? People who agree with us and would be encouraged by this, or the uninitiated we would be trying to persuade?"

"Both," he said, beaming.

Charming, but not literarily sound. "A double-minded book is unstable in all its ways," I said, parodying a Bible verse that says the same about a double-minded person. I had always written to a single audience at a time, and I urged Dr. LaHaye to choose one.

He wanted to encourage believers and persuade unbelievers, a lofty—if unrealistic—goal. I was confident that, by the time I sat before the computer, I would have persuaded Dr. LaHaye to pick one audience.

Dr. LaHaye and I parted that day agreeing that I would run with the idea and attempt to create a sample first chapter and synopsis that Rick could shop to publishers. Dr. LaHaye would serve as theological expert and prophecy consultant and would not attempt to co-write. I would defer to him on the theology, and he would defer to me on the writing. If the thing sold, we'd split everything fifty-fifty, minus Rick's commission, of course.

The hint that we might be producing something special came from the fact that the sample chapter alone kept drawing me back to the keyboard. This was a story I had heard and told all my life and that had always fascinated me. If you're supposed to write what you know and what you would read, this was up my alley. Like many writers, I have often cautioned wannabes: No one really *likes* to write; they like to *have written*. That idea is not, of course, original, but I sure identify with it. Writing is hard work, especially when the sheen of the novelty of the idea has been worn dull by the daily obligation to produce pages.

But this, like only a few of my previous works of fiction, proved a labor of love. I couldn't wait to get back to it every day. The only niggling question was whether people who had been raised with this story, as I had been, would be intrigued enough to stay with it when they knew the end. What kept me going was that I loved old stories told new. It was the telling that made the difference, and if that was strong enough, the knowing didn't have to get in the way.

I finally produced about ten pages that Dr. LaHaye and Rick and I were happy with. Rick immediately circulated that prototype first chapter to ten or twelve publishers, half of whom passed for various reasons. Some just didn't think it would work, while others feared that, with two widely published authors and an agent attached, the price would likely be prohibitive. (One of my favorite memories is of one publisher who—when told that two others had already offered twice what he proposed—said, "If you can get that for this, you'd better take it." This is not a Christian thought, so forgive me, but I do wonder what he'd say today.) The publishers who expressed interest were apparently intrigued enough to not care that their offer would be split three ways.

It came down to two publishers, both enthusiastically offering a $50,000 advance. Tyndale House Publishers in Illinois seemed most enthusiastic, and Rick and Dr. LaHaye and I enjoyed the story of their

First Writing Tip

While *Left Behind* became the exception that proves the rule, most experts agree that you should write to a single audience. For me that meant that, when I was writing a magazine column to readers roughly my mother's age and sharing her values, I imagined writing to her.

When I wrote sports biographies, I was writing to people just like me: somewhat knowledgeable, rabid fans. So I imagined writing to myself, writing what I would want to read.

When I write on spiritual themes to a general audience, I must take that audience into consideration too. That doesn't mean I will be condescending or judgmental. It means I imagine a friend or loved one I respect and admire, but whom I know disagrees with me on the issues.

Know where your audience is coming from, imagine someone you know or know of who fits in that audience, and pretend you're writing to that person alone. When I find myself in territory I know is sensitive and has been the subject of criticism, skepticism, or even ridicule, it's vital that I let the reader know that I know. I might even write, "I'm not stupid; I know how this sounds. But hear me out."

The key in writing *Left Behind* for an audience of believers as well as doubters and the uninitiated was to portray credible characters who represented opposing viewpoints. I included atheists, agnostics, doubters, the puzzled, the angry. I wanted characters anyone could identify with. And not all those characters came to see things my way, just as I knew that not all readers would.

president's reaction: He loved the sample chapter and the proposal, and despite being met with skepticism in house over the very issue I feared (that readers already know the outcome), he said, "I believe we could sell half a million of these."

Legend has it that some on his staff presented him with a "Pie in the Sky" plaque for that starry-eyed prediction. A couple of years later, when *Left Behind*, the first book in the series, had been averaging more than a quarter million sales a month for nearly a year (to date it is nearing nine million in sales), he considered presenting his doubters with "O Ye of Little Faith" plaques.

The truth is, despite their president's confidence, Tyndale House wisely hedged its bet. Rick Christian had presciently persuaded them to go against the grain of the Christian Booksellers Association market, which customarily releases full-length adult fiction in trade paperback form, and release *Left Behind* in hardback. So to save money, Tyndale House printed thirty-five thousand books, but just twenty-thousand jackets, because jackets cost roughly the same as the books themselves. Should it become clear that the first twenty thousand jacketed books would be all they needed, they could shred the remainders and save the expense of those other jackets.

Left Behind sold nearly ninety thousand hardbacks its first year, and we enjoyed the privilege of being able to tweak the jacket for those books sold after the first twenty thousand.

The plan was to cover the Rapture and the seven-year Tribulation period in one big book. I was halfway through the writing when I realized I had covered only two weeks. Dr. LaHaye and I called the publisher and suggested a trilogy. When, by the middle of the writing of the second book, *Tribulation Force*, I had covered only a couple of months, we agreed on a six-book series. That soon was adjusted to seven, then finally twelve. There will also be three prequels (à la the

Star Wars series) and a final sequel. I'm just glad Tyndale is not asking for one book for every year of the thousand-year kingdom.

With the phenomenon the Left Behind series became (nearly sixty-five million sold at this writing), people have asked if I felt somehow destined or chosen to write it. After riding this rollercoaster for more than ten years, I have to say that in many ways I felt prepared for it, at least. It seems an interesting confluence that brought Dr. LaHaye and me together. Though he is twenty-four years my senior and almost exactly the age of my mother, we have many things in common (we both are Michigan natives who experienced strong church influences as children; we each have enjoyed a long, happy marriage; we love sports, being grandfathers, etc.). And while, as I say, I am neither theologian nor scholar (as Dr. LaHaye is), we share a uniquely similar evangelical heritage that finds us fundamentally agreed on the issue of the Bible and prophecy.

I was raised to respect my elders, yet I especially enjoy those who can roll with my brand of humor. Dr. LaHaye is fond of saying that he believes the Rapture could occur during his lifetime. I like to say, "Then it'll have to be soon, won't it?"

Despite feeling somewhat prepared for this daunting task—doing justice to the greatest cosmic event that could ever occur—and having worked with many high-profile people (not to mention having written scores of books), I still vividly recall the feeling when I sat before the blank computer screen to write Left Behind in 1995.

Determined to honor Dr. LaHaye's vision, committed to doing justice to the biblical record of the prophecies, and aware of the magnitude of the story, I was overwhelmed.

I told myself I had done this before, written many novels for kids and adults, knew this story, believed it, and should be ready to tell it. But I was also awash in doubt, painfully aware of the poverty of the personal resources I brought to the table. I don't want that to come across as false humility. In many ways I did feel I was the right person for the job. But without an audience—a single reader—to imagine, and with the scope of the narrative looming, I was a candidate for a big-league bout with writer's block.

Problem was, I didn't believe in writer's block and had been saying so to budding writers for years. My idea went like this: Writing may be art and craft, but it is also your job. Factory workers and executives don't get to call in and say "I have worker's block today." They would be told to get their behinds into the workplace or look for another job.

I have a sign that reminds me: "The only way to write a book is with seat in chair."

And so there I sat.

People have asked if God gave me the words. No, I don't claim to write the words of God. I don't write Scripture. But I am not ashamed to say I could only pray and confess that I needed help. I felt inadequate to the task, but I never considered shirking the responsibility. It was an honor, a gift. I simply didn't want to get in the way of it.

My father, who passed in 2003, always told my brothers and me that there were two kinds of people: those who tried to see how little they had to do to get by, and those who did whatever it took to accomplish their tasks. "So many people just slide along," he would say, "that if you merely do your job, you will stand out."

Well, with my crisis at the keyboard, I wasn't thinking about standing out. I just wanted to somehow muster the courage to dive into a difficult task. But with Dad's counsel echoing in my brain, I did what countless writing gurus have advised for years: I simply started putting words on the screen.

My dad was raised in poverty by a single mom and became a celebrated police chief. I could certainly write a novel based on someone else's great idea. Within minutes I was engrossed in the story and hoped readers—first, of course, Dr. LaHaye—would be too.

How could I have known it would change my life, make publishing history, but best of all, somehow cross over into the general market (proving that Dr. LaHaye's dual-audience instincts, while unconventional, were dead on), and change readers' lives too?

It's been quite a ride, but it seems to me the journey is more instructive than the destination, so let me start when making a living as a writer was merely a dream.

CHAPTER
1

Early Breaks

It shouldn't surprise me, but it amuses me when people ask if I've written anything besides the Left Behind series. I'm tempted to say "No, I hit pay dirt on the first try."

Left Behind was not my first book. It was my 125th. The fact that it alone has outsold all the rest of my books put together (except its own sequels, of course) is another matter.

***

I would probably never have picked up a pen if I hadn't been such a sports nut. I am a huge fan of all sports and have been since childhood, but baseball was my first love. The Little League baseball team I played on finished fourth in the state (Michigan) in 1961 and then first in 1962, and we missed going to Williamsport, Pennsylvania, for the Little League World Series by one game. The team that knocked us out of the tournament went on to finish second in the world. I still remember most of the details and the score of every game. That's how we fanatics are.

Before I explain how sports led me into writing, let me assure you that you don't have to be a sports fan to get something out of this chapter. The point is that I turned one passion into another, and you can too. My first seventeen or eighteen books were nonfiction, many of them as-told-to autobiographies of sports stars, and those grew out of my background as a sports writer.

As you've probably noticed, people who try to write about your area of interest without really having a background in it can never really do justice to the subject. That's why you so often hear that you should write what you know. If I had attempted aviation writing, pilots would have seen through every detail. When I read sports books, I can tell within one page whether the writer has a clue.

What's your passion? Your strength? What field do you really know? Write about it. Fashion a short story, write a poem, interview a leader in the field, or work on a novel. Put yourself and your interests into it.

If writing is hard work, becoming recognized as a writer is even harder. Writing about something you know little about will make it only drudgery. Specialize—especially during your formative writing years—in your own area of interest. Doing so will help you when the writing comes hard and the only thing keeping you at the keyboard is the dream of success.

From the age of eight, I just knew I was going to be a big league baseball player. That dream became my whole life. Baseball was my god. I ate, drank, and slept baseball. It invaded my dreams.

Every single book report I wrote in junior high was about baseball. Finally, my English teacher, Barry Dopp (who was himself a sports fan and a basketball referee), said I had to pick something else for my next assignment. I selected a book with a black executive in suit and tie depicted on the cover and flashed it to Mr. Dopp. It was called *Wait*

Till Next Year and purported to tell the inspiring story of the president of coffee company Chock Full o' Nuts.

Mr. Dopp said that was fine.

He hadn't noticed that the exec on the cover was one of the most famous baseball players of all time, the man who had broken the color barrier in the big leagues: Jackie Robinson.

Fortunately, Mr. Dopp was amused, partly because he knew Jackie Robinson's story was about a lot more than baseball. For my next book review, however, he made the selection: *Roll Shenandoah*, by Bruce Lancaster. So there *was* life beyond baseball. I was transported to another time, another place, and my reading became wide and eclectic overnight.

One of the greatest gifts my parents ever gave me was a subscription to *Sports Illustrated*. I've read it religiously for more than forty years, and of course I read the sports page every day as a kid too. Despite Mr. Dopp's having broadened my outlook, I was still a baseball freak and hardly knew what to do with myself when the sport wasn't in season. I followed the other major sports too, but they never grabbed me the way baseball did. To help feed my hunger for the game, my father came up with a great diversion: dice baseball. The roll of the dice determined a single, double, triple, home run, walk, error, stolen base, or double play. That kept me occupied for hours. I made full season schedules, played dozens of games every day, and kept careful scores and stats on all the players.

I'd write about each virtual game as if I were a sports writer, then read aloud my clichéd, beginning prose to whomever would listen (usually only my mother). I had no idea how much this would impact my future. It was probably one of the most pivotal things that happened to me as a child. I had to have learned a little by osmosis—

some of the best writing published has been found in *Sports Illustrated*. I could hardly have had better instructors.

As I said before, big doors turn on small hinges. When I was thirteen, my father accepted a job as chief of police in a Chicago suburb and we moved to Illinois. When I broke my arm playing high school football, I got another opportunity to write. To stay close to the sports scene—and to get into the games free—I started covering our high school's games for a local newspaper. My parents had to drive me to the games, then to the newspaper office, where they sat waiting for me in the parking lot as I fashioned my stories. I was paid a dollar an inch. I have always looked older than I am (an advantage back then; not so fun now), so few could have guessed that I was a kid with a ride waiting for me outside.

I almost immediately realized I had found my niche. While my early articles were painfully amateurish, I did have a certain flair and bent toward sports writing, because of all my reading and my passion for the games.

My arm healed in time for baseball in the spring, and I eagerly returned to what I considered the center of my life. But then I injured my knee, and this was before the advent of reconstructive arthroscopic surgery. While it took a long time to admit or accept it, any future I might have had in baseball was gone.

That injury finally shook my life back into balance. I was a Christian, but had put baseball far ahead of even my faith. Now I understand that I had to forfeit the game I loved to put God back in His proper place in my life—but giving up my dream caused deep pain.

Setting my sights on a career in sports writing assuaged some of the sense of loss. I decided I wanted to be sports editor of the *Chicago Tribune* by the time I was thirty-five. I couldn't even imagine myself older than that.

Ironically, while I was already a professional writer, I was too young for the high school newspaper staff, which was open only to juniors and seniors. I began to look forward to Journalism 101 the way I had once looked forward to the big leagues. I learned to take pictures at sporting events, and by the time I was old enough to take journalism and write for the school paper, I was driving myself to games and continuing to string for local papers. Life was sweet.

To me, sports are a microcosm of life. There are rules and boundaries, referees, opponents, hot and cold streaks, errors, bad breaks, beginnings, middles, ends, onlookers.... You don't know what's going to happen next.

My journalism teacher, Richard Carey, had contacts at the *Tribune* and motivated us with the promise that if we came up with a story worthy of that big city daily, he would pass it on to the editors. And who knew? One of us might earn a byline there.

During my junior year, the buzz around school was that we were going to have a famous assembly speaker: Bob Richards. An Olympic pole vault champion, Richards had had his picture on Wheaties boxes and was now a motivational speaker. I also happened to know he was active with the Fellowship of Christian Athletes.

Mr. Carey told me that I, as sports editor of the Forest View High School *Viewer*, would get the privilege of attending a press conference with Richards and the sports editors of other high school papers in our district. I prepared a long list of questions.

Richards was inspiring at the assembly, and back in those days was allowed to speak, if obliquely, about his faith. I made a note to ask him to expand on that at the press conference. But somehow a whole lot more people than the sports editors had been invited, and I found myself in a theater with three hundred other kids. I crossed out question after question, knowing that, if I was lucky, I would get to ask just one. I narrowed it to the faith issue.

I stood and waited my turn, and finally Richards called on me. I asked him to say more about his personal faith, and he grinned broadly, apparently realizing that, since I had brought it up, he had the freedom to say what he wanted. And he had a lot to say.

I wrote that story, and Mr. Carey submitted it to the *Chicago Tribune*. They published it under the headline "High School Scribe Scores." Soon it was picked up and reprinted in a Christian youth magazine, *Campus Life* (now called *Ignite Your Faith*), and suddenly I felt like a real writer.

By age nineteen, I became the full-time sports editor of the paper I had been stringing for, and I figured I still had sixteen years to reach my goal of the same job at the *Tribune*.

But God had other ideas, as He often does.

CHAPTER 2

Change of Course

I've learned that one of the most common memories of people of faith—regardless their denomination or stripe—is of some transformational event at youth summer camp. Evangelicals like me, Catholics, Jews, people from the mainline denominations, even adults raised in eastern religions recall such events.

I spent my high school summers (which fell in the mid-1960s) at Camp Hickory in Round Lake, Illinois. During my first summer there, in the midst of all the fun and mischief, I made a life-changing decision. It was time to get serious about my faith and make it my own, rather than just an inheritance from my parents and my culture, and I was determined to live out this commitment despite any embarrassment. Lots of kids have rededication experiences that fade in the light of reality back in high school, but mine took and remains to this day.

The following summer I was deeply moved by a camp message challenging us kids to consider going into full-time Christian work. The point was made that any believer should be full-time about his faith. While those who pursue secular occupations are no less devout, some Christians are called to make their living in service to God and the church. Bottom line, I felt that call and stood to express my commitment.[1]

This was no light decision. I sensed the upheaval that might result. Was I surrendering sports writing? My *Chicago Tribune* dream? Did this mean I would give up writing altogether and become a pastor or a missionary? I didn't feel gifted in those fields. All I knew was that I felt called, had answered, and was willing.

I have learned that God often gifts people and prepares them before He calls them, which He did in my case. Five years later I was married, working full-time as a sportswriter/photographer, and growing uneasy with what was happening in professional sports. The big money days were beginning, and pro sports soon became business rather than fun and games—and so did sports writing.

One day I caught a glimpse of a reflection of myself in a store window and saw a twenty-one-year-old man in a suit and tie. I felt old. And it struck me: It was time to make good on that commitment I'd made at camp five summers before.

When I started looking for work in Christian publishing, my colleagues thought I was nuts. They knew I was a Christian, but they couldn't imagine that writing and publishing in the religious arena would be anything but deadly boring.

I soon landed a job as editor of a high school Sunday school paper for Scripture Press Publications in Wheaton, Illinois, and began there late in 1971. The weekly publication, *FreeWay*, which was produced in thirteen-issue quarterly packets, focused on first-person as-told-to stories. I bought or assigned many of these stories, but I had to write

[1] In 2003, I wrote an article for *Christian Camping International* magazine about my camp experience, and it won first place for first-person article from the Evangelical Press Association. You can read that article on pages 215-223.

more than half of them. That meant traveling all over the country, interviewing, and writing people stories in the voice of my subjects. It was like journalism boot camp, and I had the time of my life.

As editor of the little paper, I also had to quickly learn all the technical aspects of publishing. I wrote the headlines and captions, did the layout, worked with the artists and photographers, even decided where page numbers went.

My boss there was Stanley C. Baldwin, a quiet, unassuming, interesting character who was also a local pastor. He not only edited everything I wrote, but he second-edited everything I edited. A college dropout, I was now, in essence, getting a taste of graduate school. Every single day I resolved to present to Stan a piece of writing or editing he couldn't improve. And every day the work returned to my inbox bearing his marks showing the things I had missed.

His eagle eye made me work harder and harder, and while I never got to the point where he couldn't change a thing (a good lesson—we all always need another pair of eyes on our work), over the course of two years I saw fewer and fewer adjustments coming back.

Working under Stan was the best schooling I ever got. I became a ferocious self-editor, and I still work to polish my writing with each pass. My goal to this day is to submit the cleanest manuscripts I can. The most gratifying thing I can hear from a publisher is "Our editors barely needed to touch it."

MY FIRST BOOK

Around this time, Scripture Press had just introduced a book publishing line, Victor Books, primarily to provide Christian education texts for churches. When I interviewed a young radical Christian who had been arrested in Chicago for trying to share his faith in the nightclub district (and who allegedly was hurting the strip clubs' business), the people at Victor Books asked if I would evaluate his story to see whether it was worth a book.

Sammy Tippit, who was then twenty-five years old, proved to be one of the boldest, most dynamic persons of faith I had ever met. His story had all the elements of a great autobiography, according to me and my twenty-three years of worldly wisdom. Victor Books decided they weren't really ready to branch into people books yet, but by then I had the bug. I needed to write this book.

So, without a specific publisher in mind, Sammy and I agreed to produce a manuscript. I interviewed him on tape for hours, and my mother and my wife transcribed the tapes. Sammy spoiled me, proving to be the most prepared and organized subject I would ever work with. He showed up at our sessions with outlines, sequence charts, and stories. At the time, I thought little of this. Only when I had done a couple of dozen such books with other people did I realize the treasure I had had in such an involved subject.

Once the writer has transcripts, the work has really just begun. I threw myself into the writing, shuttling pages to Sammy for approval or adjustment.

People often asked how hard it was for me to get my first book published, and I'm embarrassed that I don't have a better story, one with dozens of rejections and sleepless nights. The truth is, Victor Books passed in advance, and another publisher liked the manuscript but thought Sammy was a slightly different stripe of believer and wanted something else. That was the extent of the initial rejection.

Sammy happened to be a Southern Baptist, so I wrote the Southern Baptist publishing house, then called Broadman, and included two chapters and an outline. A couple of days later, their editor called and said they had decided to look for someone to write a Sammy Tippit book just the day before my letter arrived.

I sent the rest of the manuscript, they sent a contract, and Sammy and I split $1,250, of which I took 30 percent. The book was published in 1974 and remains in print in its fourth incarnation, as *God's Secret Agent* (Tyndale). Sammy now runs an international Christian ministry out of San Antonio, and I serve on his board. Better than that, he and I are lifelong friends. We trade grandbaby pictures by e-mail.

My wife, Dianna, and I were both working back when that first book was published, and between us we probably grossed only $16,000 a year. I began writing more and more on the side, because we wanted to start a family and agreed she would be a stay-at-home mom. I needed two sources of income.

Victor Books assigned me a couple of Christian education books— one on strategies for vacation Bible school and one on how to get through to teens. Those were tiny paperbacks that actually came out before the Tippit book, just because of the vagaries of publishing schedules. With a few book titles on my résumé, I was ready to get busy as a freelancer.

BIG BREAK

One day in 1973, Stan Baldwin asked if I'd ever heard of Hank Aaron. Well, duh. He was only the most famous baseball player on the planet, threatening Babe Ruth's seemingly unbreakable career home run record. Stan said a New York publisher had asked him to write a Hank Aaron book from an inspirational standpoint (Hank was a devout Catholic). Stan wondered if I'd like to write it with him, because of my sports writing background. Stan would concentrate on the spiritual aspect, I on the baseball.

I remember that conversation in Technicolor and surround sound, because I knew instinctively that if this partnership actually happened, it could change my life. Listing a few inspirational books on my résumé had opened a few doors in the writing field, but a Hank Aaron book could provide opportunities I had not allowed myself to even dream of.

Plus, imagine me, a lifelong baseball aficionado, merely getting the chance to meet Hank Aaron. Even if no book resulted, I would be in heaven. I had been keeping a finger in the sports world by covering high school games for the local newspaper for ten dollars an article, but to be able to write a sports book—and who knew how many more might come from that?—well, this was too good to be true.

Meeting and spending time interviewing and working with Hank Aaron was everything I hoped it would be. It was good that I had a writing partner, because at first I was so overwhelmed at meeting my childhood hero that I was speechless. Besides interviewing him on tape, we got to hang with him for a few days, tagging along on commercial shoots and personal appearances, and just enjoying meals together.

When I finally found my voice, my obsession with baseball helped us bond a bit, and he seemed genuinely surprised that I understood the game and remembered what to most people would be trivial details. He especially appreciated that I remembered specific feats of his.

I'll never forget being there when someone naively asked him if he had "ever gone through an entire game without hitting a home run."

Hank raised a brow at me and said, "Man, I've been oh-for-August."

Bad Henry was published by Chilton in 1974 (the use of *bad* to mean "great" had just become fashionable), and as I suspected, it opened doors for which I had no other key.

Many years later, a series of unusual coincidences saw me hurrying to an errand in Atlanta, and who should I run into but Hank Aaron himself? When I called his name, he gave one of those weary nods that celebrities give to anyone who shouts out their name as they pass. I said, "Jerry Jenkins. I wrote your book."

That book was just one of many written about Aaron, and the years had changed us both, so I was relieved when he immediately broke into a smile and greeted me warmly. I don't know what I'd have done if he had had to rack his brain for that memory.

In 1973, I asked Pat Williams if he would let me shop the idea of a book about him to publishers. In the early 1970s I had written a magazine story about him, then the youngest general manager in the history of pro sports (GM of the Chicago Bulls basketball team at twenty-nine years old). Holman published *The Gingerbread Man* in 1974, and Pat and I became lifelong friends, doing several other books together. (He's now senior vice president of the Orlando Magic and one of the country's leading motivational speakers.)

At the same time, Dick Motta, a most interesting character, was coach of the Bulls. My sports writing background, my growing list of similar credits, and my work on the Aaron book helped place a deal for a book on Motta with Chilton. I'll never forget the Chilton editor traveling to Chicago and meeting with Dick Motta and me at a local hotel. As we chatted the project through, the editor said, "I'm thinking of advancing you five each."

Before I could stop myself, I blurted, "Thousand?" my voice cracking. Real professional. He smiled and nodded. That may not sound like much today, but that was nearly half my salary.

The Motta book proved great fun, because the National Basketball Association was still in its infancy then. Two nights in a row I sat right next to Motta on the team bench at the old Chicago Stadium and followed him into the locker room at halftime and after the games. That wouldn't happen today, and what a taste of the sport it gave me. I heard every comment, listened in on team huddles, witnessed the interactions between coaches, players, officials—even heard what went on between opposing players on the court.

Stuff It (give me a break; it's a basketball term) resulted in my only writing-related injury. (All right, that's stretching it. The injury resulted from my own stupidity.) I got word that the book was featured in the window of the famous Kroch's & Brentano's bookstore on Michigan Avenue in the Chicago Loop. By then I had left Scripture Press, enjoyed a short tenure as editor of *Inspirational Radio/TV Guide,* and become the twenty-five-year-old managing editor of a publication with a circulation of more than three hundred thousand: *Moody Monthly,* the magazine of the Moody Bible Institute in Chicago.

I couldn't wait until my lunch break to make the one-mile trek and see my book in that window. Problem was, I weighed more than three hundred pounds at the time, and high-heeled shoes for men were de rigueur. (I don't know what we were thinking; garish patterns and lapels that could apply for statehood completed the look.) That fast lunch-hour round-trip so injured my feet that for six weeks I limped around in moccasins.

By 1974, my income from freelance writing was soon matching my salary, and Dianna and I were getting more serious about starting a family. In the course of my work over the past six months, however, I had interviewed several middle-aged men (all about twice my age) and believed God was trying to tell me something.

Though these men's stories were totally disparate, during the interviews I asked each if he had any regrets at the current stage of his life. To a man, each said he wished he'd spent more time with his kids during their growing-up years. I discussed this with Dianna and said, "If I reach their age with the same regret, I'll be without excuse."

So we decided on a policy: Once we had children, I would bring home no work from the office and would not write from the time I got home from work until the time the kids went to bed. More on that policy later, as it proved to have a dramatic effect on our home life.

INTERVIEWING TIPS

I learned a lot from the dozens and dozens of first-person as-told-to stories I've written. First, I learned tricks and techniques to make the good recordings essential for accurate and complete transcripts, my single most important source of information and the lifeblood of any biography.

A tiny piece of hardware dramatically improved the fidelity of my recordings and resulted in much more usable transcripts. The gadget is called a Y-clip and fits into the microphone jack of a recorder, allowing you to run two microphones at the same time. I recommend lapel mikes (with long cords) clipped somewhere under your chin and the chin of your subject. These small mics are soon forgotten, eliminating the intimidation factor. You'll be amazed at the sound quality.

Always take an extension cord so you can reach an outlet. You can bring all the batteries you want, but the first time they malfunction, you'll thank me for advising that you come equipped for AC power every time.

Another gadget that will save your hide: a cheap ear piece. Attach it to the recorder and stick it in the ear farthest from your subject. You will then hear your subject live in one ear and the recording in progress in the other. You won't miss a word, and you'll be able to tell instantly if the recorder cuts out, skips, stops, or malfunctions in any way.

If you're using cassettes, look for the knockout tab that makes it impossible for you to record over something you have already taped.

Working With Celebrities

I don't recall whether I learned this somewhere or it was just something I understood intuitively, but early on in my season of working with people in demand, I established a policy: I would not ask them for anything other than what the publisher was paying them for. They had already committed to giving me large blocks of uninterrupted time for interviews, and also shadowing time, when I just hung in the background and watched them interact with their families, teammates, the press, and colleagues. This helped me catch their natural voice, which was often different from their interview voice.

I noticed that almost all the other people in their lives had an agenda, something they wanted. People hinted at what they wanted, or came right out and asked for pictures, pennants, autographs, tickets, or even to have the celeb call a relative and wish him happy birthday. I decided I would not do that, and to my surprise, they noticed and appreciated it.

I asked for only their time, for which they were being handsomely paid, but I did not otherwise have my hand out, asking for or expecting anything. That helped when friends asked me to ask them for such things. I'd say, "You know what? I don't even ask for those things for myself or my sons."

In almost every instance, at some point the person himself or a manager or agent would contact me and say, "I noticed you didn't ask for anything. Can we send you some pictures for your kids? Would you like a few tickets to a game?" Now it was time to gratefully accept. The last thing I wanted was to leave a memory of myself as just another moocher.

Remove this tab immediately after recording the second side of a tape. The first time you realize you've turned a tape over twice and are still using it, erasing the first side as you go, you'll wish you'd followed this advice.

And remember, until they are transcribed, your recorded tapes should be considered unique and priceless (they are both, and you don't want to have to start over). Treat them as treasured stuff.

The second thing I learned is that you have to put people at ease. Some of my subjects are intimidated by the tape recorder, even though it is no longer one of those big reel-to-reel jobs. I assure interviewees that the recording is not for broadcast and that it is unlikely anyone else—except the transcriptionist—would ever hear the tape. (When I do ask someone else to transcribe a tape, I ask that he reproduce every word. Yes, there's a lot of repetition, but I don't want to risk losing a thing.) When I do my own transcribing, I edit as I go, leaving out chunks if I know I won't ever use them.

I keep the Record button locked on and use the Pause button when I want to ask or say something off the record. Your transcriptionist doesn't need to hear you asking where the bathroom is, and he doesn't need to listen in on a phone conversation that interrupts the interview.

I also use the Pause button to subtly indicate to the subject that I know the interview is not about me. It's important to bond with your subject, maintain eye contact, nod, look puzzled or curious—whatever you need to keep him going. When a story reminds you of one from your own life and there is value in saying so, conspicuously hit the Pause button before saying "I know exactly what you mean, because when I was nine, I got separated from my parents, and I'll never forget how I felt when I thought ..." Your interview becomes a conversation, but the subject knows it's his story being recorded, not yours too.

I also recommend assuring interviewees that, while you will handle all the writing, they will have full veto power over every word—and that is the phrase I use. There is no equivocating: "My job is to capture the essence of what you're saying, and even more importantly, to make you sound like you, so you will have full veto power over every word. If it doesn't sound like you, if I use a word you wouldn't use, or—primarily—if I have somehow misunderstood and misrepresented you, you can correct it. Of course not one word will go to the publisher until you have approved it."

Of course full veto power applies only to as-told-to articles and books. While it always aids in accuracy to at least check back with someone on their quotes (even *Time* and *Newsweek* have extended me that courtesy), you would offer full veto power only to a subject whose name will appear as the author, à la *by Fred Interviewee as told to Jerry B. Jenkins.*

As you gain experience, you will find that some subjects find it off-putting when you show up with a sheaf of papers or a yellow pad filled with questions. Doing so seems to indicate that you think you know everything you need to know already, and that you wish to determine the course of the conversation. It is one thing to be prepared and make it clear to the subject that you have done your homework, but quite another to create the impression that you know everything about the subject, or that you have a knowledge of the person's area of expertise that matches his own. You're there so *he* can enlighten *you.*

That said, nothing is more annoying to a subject—especially a busy, visible, well-known one—than having to rehash commonly known facts about himself.

Pore over all the previously published stuff you can find about your subject, including publicity materials provided by his people. If there's an anecdote you want to examine, by all means ask for more detail.

But if you merely want to confirm details (a person's background, date of birth, education, work history, awards, etc.), you might just quickly read him a list and say, "I assume that's all accurate." If it's not, he can correct you.

Rather than create a list of questions, I jot down four major areas of discussion on a small sheet of paper, maybe even just the back of an envelope. I might start with childhood and family relationships, move to significant events, then to career and adulthood. Let the questions you ask grow from the answers you hear. That tells your subject you're listening and willing to let the story go where it will.

Try not to be too intimidated by your subject. The first time I interviewed Billy Graham for *Inspirational Radio/TV Guide*, I was twenty-four years old and so thrilled to be in his presence that I couldn't help daydreaming of bragging about it. We had been discussing how, during his first pastorate, his church had to carefully budget to add a radio program to their expenses. I decided to ask whether the radio station extended a wire all the way to the church or he had to go to the station to broadcast the program. But he finished his previous answer by saying, "Ruth and I were so poor that we didn't eat meat but once a week."

And I forgot my question.

So, I said, "Well, then, ah, what *did* you eat?"

He gave me a puzzled look, as if to ask what that could possibly have to do with anything, then said, "Well, bread and pasta and that sort of thing."

He could see I was no Mike Wallace.

MY FAMILY POLICY

Even before our kids came along, my wife and I set a policy that prohibited me from bringing home any work from the office and from doing any writing from the time I got home from work until the time the kids went to bed. (Of course, sometimes we put them to bed at four-thirty.)

May I play schoolmarm for a moment? I'm a grandfather in his late fifties, so maybe that earns me the right to be heard. My initial motivation for the policy was that I didn't want to reach middle age with the same regrets as many of the middle-aged men I had interviewed for my books. I had an inkling that the time I invested in our sons would benefit them in their lives, but I had no idea that much of the benefit would be mine.

By maintaining this family policy while I was a magazine editor, then publisher, then book publisher, then finally a vice president for publishing, I pushed my only available freelance writing time to late at night. I don't need any pats on the back, but it was a sacrifice. My wife and I were old-fashioned enough to believe a mother needed to be home with the kids during their formative years, and so I still needed two sources of income. I couldn't just give up the writing for more than a decade.

I had to rise early to beat the traffic from the suburbs into Chicago every day, so I had to be in bed no later than midnight. That meant my writing window was roughly from nine to midnight during my sons' early years.

I'm not a night person, but I had no choice. It's amazing how much you can get done when you have only three-hour blocks. Believe it or not, I was more productive during those years, in terms of the number of pages produced and books published, than I have ever been since—even after going freelance full time in 1990.

The major benefit to me as a writer? No guilt. I told my kids they were my top priority, and if I had made that a lie by always being busy when they were around, I'd have written under a burden of guilt.

Kids—and spouses—hear what you say, but they believe what you do. Maintain your priorities, and your work will benefit.

Every day, I logged between two and three hours with the kids. And we didn't have to be discussing the meaning of the cosmos. Sometimes all they wanted was to climb on me. We played outside. We played inside. We were friends. I was a novelty to the rest of the neighborhood kids, because they rarely saw their fathers at all, let alone outdoors.

Other fathers had fallen for the myth of quality time. It went like this: If you spent quality time with your kids, you didn't necessarily have to spend a large quantity of time.

But to kids, quality is quantity. The talkative kid wants to talk. The quiet one wants to be quiet. The little one wants attention. Invest the time, and they all get what they need.

I would not have missed those growing-up years for anything. I prayed with my boys, played with them, sat with them, watched them, listened to them, put them to bed every night. It was a ritual. Dianna had them all day; I had them once I got home. She needed her time, and we needed time to date and continue to court each other. Our kids saw that too, and they tell me now that it gave them a tremendous sense of security.

I was there, hearing it firsthand, when the boys said precious things at tender ages. Our youngest son, Mike, said his elementary school basketball team had lost, "but it wasn't fair because one kid on the other team had hair under his arms."

I said, "That *doesn't* seem fair; how old was he?"

"They said he was only twelve," Mike said, "but that he's already been through poverty."

I guess poverty will put hair under your arms.

Middle son, Chad, wanted me to weigh him when he was five years old, so I put him on the scale and told him what he weighed. Then he said, "Let's see how much you weigh, Dad."

As I've said, back then I weighed more than a hundred pounds more than I do today. (I got tired of having a driver's license that read: "Photo continued on other side.")

I stepped on the scales and we watched the numbers whiz by. Chad said, "Hey, Dad, you weigh all of it!"

He was always good for a line or two. On his fifth birthday, I urged him to eat all the beans he had piled on his plate. He said, "Dad, by the time I eat all these, I'll be six."

He asked me how old Able was when Cain murdered him. I said, "I don't think we know that, Chad."

He said, "In my Bible he lived for eight verses."

Eldest son, Dallas, when he was about six, was playing with a Star Wars action figure under the kitchen table and didn't realize Dianna and I were in the next room and could hear every word. He was lecturing the action figure. He said, "You may die in this mission. You don't want to go to hell, because Satan's mean and he won't give you anything. But if you go to heaven, you can ask Jesus for anything you want. And if it's all right with your mom, He'll give it to ya."

Dianna especially appreciated the theology of that.

The point is, I would not have wanted to hear any of those stories secondhand. They are treasured memories. And logging all that time with the boys made their teen years a lot easier—at least for us. None of our boys rebelled or went counterculture on us. They went through the typical stages when they decided they knew more than we did. They were probably right. I told them, "I can be right only about half the time, so you may be correct when you question me. But I still have to live with the decision."

Dianna and I realized a few years ago that while the boys often questioned our judgment, they never questioned our motives. How could they? We had put in the time, proving their value to us.

Why do I tell you that?

Because there are things more important in this world than your writing career. The Bible asks, what does it profit people who gain the whole world and lose their own soul? What joy would there have been in my writing bestselling novels if it had cost me my family to do it?

Maintain your priorities and your writing will benefit.

CHAPTER 3

Why Write?

I don't know why you write. I have only an idea why *I* do. Most people are gifted in some area or another. I'm not taking about being a gifted student, as in having a high IQ. I'm talking about having an innate knack for certain things.

At the risk of sounding falsely modest, I truly believe I have been given only one gift, and that is a knack for writing. That doesn't mean I was brilliant at it and didn't need a lot of training and experience. In fact, I'm one who believes that no writer ever arrives. Yes, after all the writing I've done and taught over the years, I should be better at it than I've ever been. But I fear that if I'm not growing, I'm stagnating. There's no reaching one level and staying there. And so I read everything there is to read about the craft, listen carefully to colleagues and idols, and try to keep expanding my knowledge and learning.

While I had a bent toward certain sports, and some people think I am instinctively funny, writing is my only gift, and so I have felt compelled to use it. If I could also sing or dance or preach, I probably wouldn't write so much.

My earliest recollection of someone talking about writing as a profession is from third grade or so, when a smart girl named Lorraine answered the teacher's what-do-you-want-to-be-when-you-grow-up question with "A journalist."

I didn't want to admit—especially to Lorraine—that I didn't know what that was. To me, writing was penmanship. And I wanted to be a big league baseball player when I grew up.

I got the sense from Lorraine's being a voracious reader and carrying around notebooks full of her own writing that journalism was something she loved the way I loved baseball. Perhaps she's a journalist today.

Some people write for the money, but statistics show that only one in a hundred writers makes a full-time living at writing. Those who love writing stick with it regardless. Those for whom the money itself is the goal are in more lucrative professions by now.

I've heard people say you should write only if you have to, are compelled to, can't imagine yourself not writing. And I know people who seem to have that bent. They would write for free if they had to. I have been asked when I knew I loved writing. My immediate answer surprised even me: "Oh, I've never loved it. Writing itself is way too hard to love. What I really love is being a writer."

That was an overstatement, of course, but it's being able to write (which is, frankly, somewhat unique) that appeals to me. (I know, you're not supposed to put a qualifier before the word *unique*, but being a writer does not make me unique. It makes me somewhat unique, and that's enough for my fragile ego.)

Being a writer soon became what I wanted to do with my life. And though the work (the actual seat-in-chair writing) is hard and rarely fun, the more I do it, the better I get at it and the more writing muscles and tools I develop. And there is that rush at the end of a productive day that makes me look back on it as if it might have actually been fun.

What I'm saying, however, is that I do not fall into the category of those who say, "I write because I can't *not* write." I admire those people, and sometimes wish I were one of them.

AM I A WRITER?

You may be so new to the writing game that you're unsure even what to call yourself. Are you a novice? A beginner? It doesn't matter. You are what you say you are. If you have decided to be a writer, you're a writer, published or not. We all have to start somewhere. Beginners often lament that the door is closed except to the big names. But think about it: Who were the big names before they were published? Nobodies.

Get serious about your career by declaring yourself a writer. Do it now, and don't look back. If doing so makes you waver or doubt yourself, maybe you're not cut out for writing. If you're looking for reasons to quit, there are plenty. If you are determined to write no matter what, you're what the publishing world is looking for.

Your results will mirror your commitment. Put in the necessary time and do the rewrites to make your own success inevitable. Make your own breaks. That's what separates hobbyists from real authors. Study, do the research, develop a thick skin, work hard, learn to take editing, and learn to edit yourself. Have you arrived yet? Neither have I.

ONLY YOUR BEST

Don't try to write a bestseller or be a modern-day Shakespeare. Simply write your best. Take chances. Push. Make bold moves. Trying to talk a publisher into an advance figure I could bounce off a pro athlete or his agent was not easy, but I wouldn't have forgiven myself if I hadn't tried. And then tracking down the player or his rep and pushing until I got a yes or no proved worth it much of the time.

If you're committed to being the best you can be, you'll achieve your best. If you're halfhearted, you'll be only that. I'm not saying that if you commit yourself 100 percent, you'll sell a million copies, but I can promise you'll be the best writer you can be.

How bad do you want to be the best you can be? If you're put off by distractions, you'll find more than you need. You have responsibilities, bills, people pulling on you; you have enemies, friends, and bosses. Ultimately, you have priorities. Decide what's important to you. You will always make the time to do what you really want to do.

If your goal is to be the best you can be, you can arrive there every day. Let's say you've never written or published anything. The best you can do without any experience, without having an in with the editor, without running on the inside track, is to just turn on your computer and start keyboarding—cranking out the pages you need to meet your daily production goals. Decide what you want to write and do it.

The next day you might come up with a great idea, but find your writing is loose. That's okay, if it's the best you can do. If you've never written anything before, start by writing a sentence. Then write a paragraph. Each paragraph needs to hold together, to make sense. Master the paragraph and then write a whole page.

SUCCESS

When I agree to do a piece of writing, even a column for a free newsletter, I give it my all, the same as I do for a book with a seven-figure

Humility

Don't ever apologize for wanting to be published. Get your work out there. Sure, a certain amount of ego is at play. Who doesn't want to be known, to be successful, to see her name in print? You simply need to remember that publishing has to be a *byproduct* of your writing, not the end goal. If you set out to glamorize yourself, write a bestseller, score, whatever you call it, you might enjoy a short-lived celebrity, but you won't have a career. As Dean Koontz has taught, the purpose of writing is communication, and if what we write is not read, that purpose is not fulfilled.

The most attractive quality in a person is humility. Sometimes money and fame will come whether or not you expect or seek them. But if you become enamored with the trappings of success, they become your passion. You need to return to your first love.

Why are you a writer?

Are you an inspirational writer?

The answers to those questions should have nothing to do with yourself. If God and others are not the reasons you write, you might as well write solely for the general market. That doesn't mean everything you write has to be a sermon or packed with scripture, but your unique worldview should come through.

advance. Regardless of the payment, my name will appear on the piece, and I don't want the reader to see a difference in quality between a piece I was paid highly for and a piece I did for less.

Don't let success or pressure change you. If you become a success, stick with what got you there. When a baseball team gets to the World Series—especially for the first time in a long time—there's often a tendency to do things differently in the series games, to raise the bar, push to new heights. The players in the lineup are juggled, a surprise starting pitcher is thrown in. The players feel the pressure to improve their games, as if throwing harder, swinging faster, or running with more abandon is the key to victory. The real key, however, is to keep doing what they did to get there.

The same can happen to a writer. You have a bestseller and you start thinking you *have* to succeed with the next one too so you aren't embarrassed or seen as a fluke. You try to blow the doors off to stay on the bestseller charts. But what does that mean? Imitating the elements you think made the difference? Can you write faster, harder, more enthusiastically? Should you write standing up?

Publishers face the same temptation. With more advance and promotion dollars committed to a bestselling author's new book, they sometimes feel the pressure to have more spoons in the soup, more people from more departments with more input into the content. In my case, I needed to stick with what worked. What we all need is a deep breath and a decision to keep doing what we've been doing, assuming it will work again.

The fact is, the market makes or breaks sales. Neither author nor publisher has much say or control over how many books sell. What you *can* control is how you write your next book. Work to your potential and let the results go. The best you can be may not put you on the critics' short list. If you try to write with a certain sales goal in mind, you're playing games. That would be pure presumption.

Who could ever have foreseen the success of the Left Behind books? It would have been pointless for me to have attempted to forecast sales based on the past. And doing so wouldn't have helped me write the books I needed to write. "A man's heart plans his way, but the Lord directs his steps" (Proverbs 16:9).

NOT LUCK, BUT PURPOSE

I don't believe in luck. I believe in faithfully, steadily paying your dues. Doing so often puts you in the right place at the right time. You grow as a writer, and one assignment leads to another. Sorry, but there are rarely shortcuts. Tackle any project you can to grow as a writer. Eventually, you'll toughen up enough to send out your article and see what happens.

After a few rejections, a few ego scrapings, someone's going to publish something you've written. That will be huge for you. You might not make much money, but pretty soon you'll start hearing from others: "You ought to interview my sister; she has a story," or "My brother works for a newspaper, and he's looking for this kind of story." People will start to notice your writing.

Regardless of where you are in your writing journey, always strive for the freedom to write about what really matters to you. Whatever else the writing life offers, nothing compares with the dream of actually changing lives with words. And if you plan to make a life of writing, you must stand for something, have a carefully considered and lived-out worldview. Know your passion. Discover what it is that can keep you in front of that keyboard day after day. If it's money, fame, and power, you'll find yourself quitting once you have achieved those—or you'll have found that you can't achieve those.

Write because you believe in something. I write because I believe that's what God wants me to do.

At a recent Christian Writers Guild reception, someone insightfully asked, "What did you have to sacrifice to have the writing career you've had?"

I had to think about that one, because the rewards have far outweighed any sacrifices. As I've said, one thing I was not willing to give up was my family—time with my kids and my wife. I've seen people do that. Until they have enough work or success to write full time, they work full time and write part time. Something has to give, usually the family. The writer is behind a closed door, or a book, or a computer screen, in essence telling her family they rank lower than writing in her list of priorities.

So what did I give up by relegating my freelance career to late nights? A little privacy. Some television. Some sleep. Was it worth it? You decide.

Q & A WITH JERRY

Why is fiction your first love?

There is something unique about fiction; not a lot of people can do it well. People who write nonfiction have an especially difficult time making the shift. I guess I'm a storyteller at heart. I also find fiction easier and more fun than nonfiction.

I have learned, however, that there is no shortcut around the research. Novelists who think fiction is easier because they can just make up everything soon find readers dissatisfied.

Jesus used fiction; His parables were clearly fictitious stories used to tell truth with a capital T.

What would be your advice to someone just getting started? Should she take any assignment just to keep writing?

Within reason. I did. I wanted to be a professional writer. I've never apologized for writing to supplement my income. It's hard to get work as a freelancer, especially to get enough so you can survive on that alone. Until you become known, people aren't calling you, you're calling them. If somebody calls with an assignment, that's a bonus. Unless it violates your sense of values, I'd take it.

Why write if you don't like writing?

Because it's me. It's what I do. Beginners like the idea of being an author, but not the hours it takes to get the job done. Lots of people want to be novelists, to make up stories people like to read. Some pretend they could do it if they only had the time.

I won't deny there are perks to being a writer, and there were even before I wrote bestsellers. Mostly I enjoy the freedom of setting my own hours and being my own boss. I don't think there's anything else I'd rather do—unless I could play big league baseball.

It's not that I hate going to the keyboard, but I put it off, dreading the encounter, especially getting started. When I finally get to it, I often think, *This isn't so bad.* Then the story draws me in, and I'm off and running.

I don't know anyone who sits at the computer with a grin thinking, *This is the most fun I've had all day. I'd rather do this than play.*

Have you ever rejected a big contract offer because it violated your personal convictions?

Absolutely. In fact, more than once. A few years ago I was presented with a novel series idea that would have been my biggest deal ever to that point. I warmed to the idea quickly, even though it wasn't mine. We talked, negotiated, settled, and signed. But it didn't grow on me as ideas often do. Often I can gauge the potential success of an idea by how much I think about it during my free time. This one just sat there.

I didn't get any peace until I decided I couldn't do it, despite the huge check already in my account. I sent the money back. I'd like to think I would have done that even if I had really needed the money. I couldn't write a story that didn't captivate me, not for any amount of money or what I could have done with it.

Is there anything wrong with ghostwriting?

If the definition of ghostwriting is writing something for someone else and receiving zero credit for it, I've done it—five times. And I have changed my mind about it. I wouldn't do it again and don't recommend it. The writer deserves credit, and the reader deserves to know who did the writing. Ghostwriting is common in publishing, especially in the inspirational market. I urge writers to insist on a byline, even if their name appears in smaller type after a *with* or an *and*. But true ghostwriting, where the writer is not mentioned? No. It's disingenuous on the part of the subject and the publisher. And besides, crediting the writer on the cover does not lessen the impact of the name of the subject. The average reader focuses on the well-known name anyway.

Chris Fabry, a trusted colleague, wrote Left Behind: The Kids from book six through forty. I lobbied for years to get his name on the cover where it is now. My dear friend Norman Rohrer, the man who founded the Christian Writers Guild in 1965, wrote *These Will Not Be Left Behind*, although my name and Dr. LaHaye's name also appear on the cover. I asked Tyndale House Publishers to double the size of Norm's name on the cover. To me it's still embarrassing to have Dr. LaHaye's and my name bigger than Norm's, but at least it's clear he did the work.

Do writers care about the quality of their work as much as they once did?

Frankly, I worry more about the quality of editing today. When I worked for *Moody* magazine, we evaluated every word and edited and rewrote as heavily as necessary. Readers could sense that care in every piece. We stood behind each word, trying to make the articles sing.

Book publishers who care do the same thing. Editors work with authors for months until the flab is gone.

I'm alarmed at the obviously thin editing in too many books, both inspirational and general. I believe writers want to get better. That's why good editors are important. The Christian Writers Guild is trying to help publishing houses (and their editors) by teaching people to write well.

Can literature have meaning and conviction even if there aren't rules anymore?

The market has a way of winnowing the drivel. There will always be room for the avant-garde and the experimental, but most readers like books with beginnings, middles, and ends—things that make sense. Books that draw you in. A lot of the factors that make something read well are invisible to the reader. When I see what too many creative writing teachers find fascinating, I shake my head. I think, *Somebody told you this was good?* In almost every case, I find the writing teacher is not published.

Call me old-fashioned, but I want to understand what's on the page, just like I want to understand what's within the frame of a piece of art. I've seen people stand before a painted mess and pretend they have a clue, as if appearing to understand makes them look deep. Give me a break. (Although in some cases, I'm sure they do understand, and I'm the dolt.) I don't want to be written off as lowbrow, but when it appears my pre-school grandkids could have produced something, I'm not going to pretend otherwise.

Some of what I've read—so-called cutting-edge stuff billed as deep, new, and fresh—is nothing but obtuse writing masquerading as something other than baloney. If the writer has to explain it, it's not working. If I am compelled to read a paragraph twice, it had better be because it moved me so much that I want to, not because I have to figure out what in the world the writer is trying to say.

In the inspirational market, the major problem is flabby writing, not so much the post-modern blather found in other genres, though no doubt we'll get there soon. Here's hoping we start some trends rather than follow them, especially when it comes to quality.

Has success changed you?

That's not for me to say. Friends, family, and colleagues would be more objective. I like to think I'm the same guy I've always been. Maybe that's because what the world calls success came when I was in my forties and not in my twenties, but I'd rather think it's because by my definition of success—which is antithetical to society's view—I was already successful. I still try to be the best I can be and leave the rankings to others.

The best compliment I ever got was when I was introduced at a writer's conference by a dear old friend. He said, "A lot of you are saying 'I knew Jerry when.' I just want to say, if you knew him then, you know him now."

I do have a standing order to the people in my life who hold me accountable. I tell them that if I ever start acting like I deserve any of this largess, they should just punch me in the mouth.

I'm not going to deny enjoying what success has wrought in my life. My family and I are more mobile, have more freedom, are able to see our loved ones almost at will. But I feel a tremendous amount of accountability and responsibility, knowing I will one day answer for what I have done with my time and resources.

Suddenly having more doesn't make you a better person. Rather, it shows who you really are. If you weren't already generous, you aren't likely to become more so when you have money. Money magnifies. What would it magnify in you? If you are cold, you'd appear colder. Warm, warmer. Nice, nicer. Mean, meaner. Beware.

WALTER PAYTON

We sports nuts take great pleasure in looking past the stats and scores and believing we can spot true greatness on the horizon. That's how I felt about young Chicago Bears player Walter Payton. He was fast becoming a superstar in Chicago, but I thought I foresaw national greatness. (That didn't take a genius; you'd have had to be blind to miss that Payton was something special.) I pitched a publisher and asked what the editors would pay for Payton's autobiography. It had to be a decent figure, because by now I was doing these only for a straight split.

Contemporary Books offered an advance I believed would interest Payton, so I set about trying to get to him. He lived in a modest home in a nearby suburb, so I sent a letter. No response. I tried contacting the Bears directly. They gave me his lawyer's name in the South. No response. I tried everything I knew over the next nine months, but I didn't hear from Payton or his lawyer.

Finally I finagled the lawyer's phone number from the Bears. When I reached him, I was prepared to scold him and say, in essence, "If you don't want him to do this, just say so. But please don't ignore me."

But the man astounded me. He acted as if he had been expecting my call. He said, "Nice to hear from you, Mr. Jenkins. You ready to write a book?"

Was I!

By the time I got back to Contemporary Books, they had forgotten about me and the offer. But Payton had had another great season, and Contemporary was eager to make good on the original deal. They dealt directly with Payton's lawyer, but when weeks went by without my seeing a contract, I started the hounding all over again. I learned that the contracts were with Walter at his home.

The lawyer gave me Payton's number, and the next thing I knew I was on the phone, hearing the incongruously high-pitched voice of the most feared running back in the National Football League. He had signed the deal, he said, all three copies, and would put them in the mail to his lawyer or the Bears.

Great. I told him I looked forward to getting together with him once the paperwork was in place. More weeks went by. The lawyer, the publisher, the Bears—none of them had heard from Walter. I called him again. Had he signed the deal? Yes. Would it help if I dropped by and picked up the signed copies? Yes.

Let me try to tell this delicately. Walter Payton was home alone. His front door was recessed into a little dark alcove. When he answered the bell, I could hear him but I couldn't see him. He was one dark man. And he had just emerged from the shower. When my eyes grew accustomed to the light, I realized he was standing there in only dark green Speedo-style briefs.

Once inside with the light on, though I knew it was impolite to stare, I realized that standing before me was one of the most incredible physical specimens I had ever seen, and that included body builders I had written about as a teenage sports writer. Payton was small by NFL standards. He was just a tick over five-foot-ten and weighed maybe 210 pounds. But his hands were massive, thicker than mine from palm to back, maybe by double.

His calves and thighs and biceps bulged like Arnold Schwarzenegger's, and it appeared that if he merely flexed his muscles, they would split his skin. "A lifter, are you?" was all I could manage, and he responded with the first of countless little fibs. He was a prankster who loved to tell tall tales.

He said, "No, I don't believe in weight training. I've never done it, never lifted." For some reason I believed him, and thought for a long time that Walter Payton had been blessed with the most dramatically sculpted body God ever created. Only when I started catching on to all his fibs did I doubt that, and when I later worked on teammate Mike Singletary's autobiography, I learned that Walter was a maniac in the weight room.

The first clue that I was being duped was when Walter produced the triple copies of the book deal; I realized he had not even read them, let alone signed them. I made sure he did that, and I took the documents to make sure they got to the proper people.

I was struck at our first interviewing session in his home by how childlike he was. That may have been where he got his nickname and I the eventual title of his book, *Sweetness*. There was a Peter Pan quality to the man, and to me it seemed his wise wife, Connie, kept him on track. He had toys all over the house: a drum set he loved to play, a pinball machine, you name it. He enjoyed watching cartoons and would switch back and forth between them and the big sporting event of the day.

Occasionally Connie would bring him a colossal meal—pork chops, mashed potatoes, gravy, sweet corn, dessert. I weighed a hundred pounds more then than I do now, and more than a hundred pounds more than Walter at the time, but he ate more than I did. I would soon learn why.

Talk about hyperactive. Walter always had to be on the move. He couldn't just sit and be interviewed. He was the original multitasker.

Once, when I came to interview him, he was busy painting his new trophy room. He just hooked the lapel mike onto his shirt and kept at it. He didn't use a ladder. He perched on a chair with a can of paint in one hand and the brush in the other, making huge, sweeping strokes. Walter was in such great shape that he didn't break a sweat or lose his breath. He painted an entire wall in just over five minutes, the whole time answering my questions. Without skipping a beat, he moved the chair and began another wall. Amazing.

One day, I drove into his subdivision at our appointed time and saw him drive past me, heading the other way. I tried to get his attention, but apparently he didn't see me. I rang and knocked, but no one was home, so I waited in his driveway for ninety minutes before heading home. We were set for the next day at the same time, so I figured something had come up or he'd just forgotten. I didn't want to waste another drive, however, so the next morning I called first. His mother answered.

She said he wasn't there, so I told her about our mix-up the day before and that I needed to get some hours in with him today. She assured me he would be home after lunch and that I should come then. I went, and we got a lot of work done. But in the middle of the interview his phone rang. In a high-pitched voice I immediately recognized, he told the caller, "No, this is his mother. He's not here right now."

I said, "You dog! I didn't talk to your mother this morning either, did I?"

He said, "Not unless you were on long distance to Jackson, Mississippi."

Another of his famous pranks was to pinch you just before a photo was shot. And I mean *pinch*. He didn't tickle, goose, or poke. He would use one of those massive hands and grab an entire butt cheek, squeezing as hard as he could. He displayed a gallery of photos of all kinds of friends and teammates and famous people, with him smiling sweetly while the person next to him wore a mask of pain and horror. He signed a copy of my photo. I had bruises on my rear for six weeks.

Once, during post-game TV interviews outside the Bears locker room, it quickly became evident from the embarrassed laughter of the reporter and crew that Walter had shown up in the nude, daring the cameramen to reveal him in all his glory.

Walter's workout routines were breathtaking. Literally. He would drive to the local high school and park at one end of the track. He would sprint a quarter mile, walk a hundred yards, sprint another quarter, walk another hundred. He kept at it until he could hardly move. Then, rather than crawl back to his car, he would push himself to run one more time around the track as hard as he could.

Walter planned it so that if he passed out, which he often did, he would end up near his car and appear to be napping, lest anyone grew concerned. When he roused, he would jog half a mile before driving home.

Often he worked out with teammates. His goal was to make them quit first, throwing up or crying. Or both. He usually succeeded.

If during the off-season he could persuade a teammate to visit him in Mississippi, he would take him to Suicide Hill, a steep embankment covered with cinders and dirt. Walter would run up and down that hill until he couldn't move anymore. Then he would recuperate and bet his teammate that he could run up and down before the other made it to the top even once. He never lost that bet.

Walter acknowledged that he had good speed, but not world-class speed. He had superhuman strength for a person his size, yet critics always wrote that he was too short, too small, or too slow. On the other hand, he held the record for the most yards gained in one game—and a career—for many years. One of his running secrets I found bizarre was that, when he knew he was about to get hit or tackled, he would purposely throw himself off balance so the opposing player might knock him back upright. Watch highlight films and you can see this happen.

Walter Payton went on to become one of the most celebrated NFL players of all time. He was Offensive Player of the Year and Most Valuable Player in both 1977 and 1985. He played in nine Pro Bowls and ran for over a hundred yards in seventy-seven different games. He once told me that the one goal he was never able to achieve was to be named Most Valuable Player one year, then improve so much for the next season that he would be named Comeback Player of the Year. He was a funny guy, but I sensed he was dead serious about that goal and disappointed he never achieved it.

Walter missed only one game in his career—due to a bruised thigh in his first season—and he went on to play 186 consecutive games. He played pro football from 1975 until 1987, and died of liver cancer in 1999 at age forty-five.

Walter will always be known as one of the greatest football players of all time because of his commitment to the task.

I learned a lot from Walter Payton about dedication to the pursuit of excellence. Have I ever pushed myself that hard, expended that much energy to test my limits? Have you?

CHAPTER 4

Keeping Your Soul Intact

Can you still be moved?

If you're a person of faith and believe you have been called to a sacred profession, that alone should move you. With a single phrase you can heal a wound or tear it open. Even today, choice words in precise order bear power unmatched by amplified images and sound and technical magic.

The following thought is not original with me, but I believe it with all that is in me: If there are no tears in the writer, there will be no tears in the reader. The emotion conjured in you as you write will be multiplied in the reader. That's good and bad. If you are breathless, he may gasp. If your lip quivers, he may weep. But if you are bored or distracted, the reader will stop turning pages.

But I'm a beginner, you say. *I don't have the confidence to write so boldly that I evoke emotion.*

At least you've put it well. Don't just show emotion. Don't write of sobbing and crying and shrieking and shaking. Show what happens and let the emotion come from the reader.

I call writing a sacred profession because I believe God chose the written word to communicate with man. In John 1, Jesus is referred to as the Word. Ephesians 4:11–12 talks about a Christian's calling, saying that Jesus Christ gave some of us to be apostles, some prophets, some evangelists, and some pastors and teachers for the equipping of the saints; a Christian believer's work is to edify of the body of Christ. Each of these roles might include writing skills. I'm no apostle or prophet, but if the definition of an evangelist is one who shares the news of Christ, I certainly want to fall into that category. And though I am not a pastor, I do teach—in classrooms and through my writing—and I hope I am, in that way, "equipping the saints."

Even if you're not of the Christian faith, consider the beauty of the words of the Bible. Psalm 91 says:

> He who dwells in the secret place of the most high shall abide under the shadow of the Almighty. I will say of the Lord, "He is my refuge and my fortress, my God, in Him I will trust."
>
> Surely He shall deliver you from the snare of the fowler and from the perilous pestilence. He shall cover you with his feathers, and under his wings you shall take refuge; His truth shall be your shield and buckler.
>
> You shall not be afraid of the terror by night, nor of the arrow that flies by day, nor of the pestilence that walks in darkness, nor of the destruction that lays waste at noonday. A thousand may fall at your side and ten thousand at your right hand, but it shall not come near you.

We live in an age of natural disasters, terrorism, broken homes, abuse, and war. Either we're overwhelmed or we're stoics who rise above every problem. We don't like to be seen as vulnerable, but isn't vulnerability far better than cynicism? The writer still capable of being moved can live a life of lasting significance. When people of the future run across your byline or some evidence of the work you left behind, your prayer should be that someone will say "Ah, yes, this was a person who could be moved, and the writing proves it."

Allow yourself to be moved, and write what moves you.

Are you moved by painful memories? I am. When our kids were little and I was maintaining my policy of giving them huge blocks of time every day, they began to take that for granted (flattering, if you think about it). They were, however, fascinated by a neighbor whose family celebrated when he got home.

He would emerge from the car and be mobbed by his wife and kids. My boys thought he must really be something special. Dianna and I knew the truth, because his wife had confided her despair. He was an alcoholic, a sex addict, and a compulsive spender. His good job was in jeopardy because he would sometimes disappear for days. The reason his family celebrated him when he got home was that they never knew when those days might be.

When my six-year-old son said, "I wish he was my dad," I had to bite my tongue. Obviously I couldn't tell him the truth. But that night, Dianna and I discussed how we had to become better friends of that couple, earn the right to be heard, try to share something with the man that would put him back on the right track. He needed an anchor in the universe.

It was already too late. The next morning I was called out of a meeting at work for a phone call from Dianna. She reported that the woman had just run to our house in hysterics, having discovered her husband in his car in the closed garage with the engine running, a suicide note on the seat. All I could think was, *Why do we always wait?*

It's been nearly a quarter of a century since that happened, yet it affects how I live, how I treat my neighbors, what I write, how I write.

If such events don't move you, don't change you, you may not be cut out for writing.

If real life reaches your core, however, you must write. Allow yourself to be deeply moved, then write out of the depth of your emotion. Before you merely gush onto the page, however, remember that if you are a beginner, you're likely not ready to publish. I never cease to be amazed at the unprofessional writing samples, e-mails, and letters that come my way. Every day I hear from people who claim they want advice and input, but they don't want to hear that they haven't a chance with an editor unless they make major revisions.

These might be people whose words could change lives, but until they edit themselves, they have little hope for publishing success. If you fear you fall into this category, I have advice that might help in your efforts to grow; see page 188.

DON'T WAIT

Many writers—or would-be writers—talk about waiting for inspiration. If you're called, inspiration and passion will permeate your writing. Don't confuse inspiration with initiative. Initiative solves your procrastination problem and pulls you through writer's block. Inspiration gives you something worth writing about.

"The very best writing is born of humility," writes bestselling author Dean Koontz. "The truly great stuff comes to life in those agonizing yet exhilarating moments when the artist is acutely aware of the limitations of his skills. For it is then that he strains the hardest to make the most he can from the imperfect materials and tools with which he must work. The purpose of writing is communication, and if the work is not read, the purpose is not fulfilled."

Real writers want to hold their printed words in their hands. If that's you, good! Go for it! Nurture that natural desire to be published. It's how you gain your voice. Frankly, when someone tells me he doesn't care to be published or paid for his writing, but that he simply wants to express himself, I don't believe it. He may be truly humble, but if his work is worth doing, his stuff worth writing, he should want it published and read as widely as possible.

FILLING YOUR RESERVOIR

To write, you need a full tank, and I'm not talking about writing resources. I'm talking about emotional and spiritual well-being. With physical exercise, anything is better than nothing. Even just five minutes on a rowing machine gets the blood pumping and the pulse jumping. The same is true with spiritual exercise; do whatever it takes to jumpstart your spiritual life—prayer, Bible reading, reflection, whatever. Don't feel like you're a failure if you haven't worked your way up to an hour a day. Anything is better than nothing—though we should, of course, be trying to build those muscles.

Some people have lamented to me that they tried to read their Bible every day or read it through in a year and got off track at some point. Others have said that they resolved to always have their nose in an inspirational or self-help book, only to find that after thirty or forty days, they missed for some reason and suddenly found themselves spiraling into old habits and giving up the quest.

That thinking—that belief that if you've slipped up, you've failed entirely—is flawed, of course. Yes, ideally we should be nurturing our souls and minds and spirits as well as our bodies every day. But missing once is no reason to crash and burn.

I used to be a victim of such perfectionist thinking. For decades I carried an extra hundred pounds, and every few years I would take a serious run at losing it. I'd eat right and start walking every day, only to quit when I missed after seventy-one straight days, allowing myself to be defeated because I had, in essence, fallen off the wagon. I don't know where such craziness comes from, but it must look as ludicrous to you as it does to me as I see it on paper here. Did my missing one day negate all I had done for those many weeks? Of course not.

I have maintained a 115-pound weight loss for three years by keeping track of everything I eat, working out, and staying vigilant. Part of the secret to this success is allowing myself to fail occasionally. Do I exceed my calorie counts sometimes? Miss a workout? Sure. I'm human. But I don't have to be perfect to succeed.

The same is true for the development of our inner lives. Feed yours. And when you forget to pray or read your Bible, or you miss church or get too busy or too lazy, just cook your soul a small meal—do just one of the things listed above—and get back on track. We can't write for other people's souls unless ours are healthy.

Q & A WITH JERRY

How do you keep your priorities—personal, spiritual, professional—in order?

I'm a compartmentalizer. I prioritize my day and do the needful things first. I work hard, but carve out time to play.

My late father was a good example; he was disciplined in every area of his life. If he made an appointment—especially with his boys—he kept it. Now that I'm self-employed and have several full-time employees, some could say I don't answer to anybody, so I can come in anytime I want and dress any way I want and do anything I want. But I feel I report to everybody, because I need to honor their expectations. My generation was raised to believe there's no short-cut for working and keeping your priorities straight.

Are you inspired to write with music playing?

No. But I do love music. All kinds. My favorite movie soundtrack is *O Brother, Where Art Thou?* which is mostly songs with lyrics, but also includes a few instrumentals. But I'm afraid I'll start singing along, so I usually write in silence and enjoy the music later. Okay, I do hum.

What Bible version is your favorite and why?

I was raised on the King James Version and now prefer the New King James because it retains the cadence of the language. When I taught our boys Bible verses, I would quote them in the King James, but I would take out the *thee*'s and *thou*'s and *ye*'s. Essentially, that's what the NKJV does. In the Left Behind series, I take the same approach. When I'm quoting the two witnesses, for instance, they sound biblical and old-fashioned, but more New King James than King James, which can come across as archaic. I also like the New Living Translation and the New American Standard versions.

Did you raise your own children on the KJV?

Yes. I remember teaching Chad the King James verse John 3:8: "The wind bloweth where it listeth, and thou hearest the sound thereof, but canst not tell whence it cometh, and whither it goeth...." He quoted it back exactly.

"Great, Chad. What does it mean?"

"Don't ask me," he said.

That's when I knew I had to translate.

Where and when do you read the Bible?

I don't limit myself. I think that any exposure to the Bible is good for me and that I should make reading it a daily devotional experience. The Word says of itself that it is alive and powerful and sharper than any two-edged sword, and that it won't return void. I used to feel guilty when I skipped a few days of devotional Bible reading. I'm over that now. Anything is better than nothing, and more is better than less.

I've also got the Bible on my computer, which gives me instant access to it all the time, whether I'm writing or not.

BILLY GRAHAM

One of the great privileges of my life was assisting Billy Graham with his memoir, *Just As I Am*. He's one of those rare people who is the same behind closed doors as in public, and ironically it's his very humility that so attracts people to him.

He is everything you would hope he would be, and more. At this writing, Mr. Graham is not well and no longer young, and it's difficult to watch him fade. But what a thrill to work with him for more than a year. Most of that time was spent in musty little offices looking at records, reports, and films. Several weeks included interviewing him in various cities and spending time with him and his wife.

Ruth Graham is one of the funniest people I have ever met. She once said: "If a husband and a wife agree all the time, one of them is unnecessary." Someone once asked if she had ever considered divorce. "Never," she said. "Homicide, but never divorce."

Once, while Mr. Graham and I were taping at their home atop Black Mountain in Montreat, North Carolina, Ruth kept correcting him from another room. "Now Bill," she'd call out, "that wasn't 1949, that was 1951. And it wasn't Boston, it was Cleveland."

Mr. Graham would roll his eyes. Finally, he said, "Ruth, would you just let me handle my own memoirs?"

"I would," she said, "but they're starting to sound like your forget-oirs."

Ruth supervised the building of that home while Mr. Graham was in Europe for several weeks during the 1950s. She bought up old shacks and had the centuries-old wood carted to the building site. Working with the architect, she designed a rustic, rambling place that was ancient the day it was finished because of the age of those boards.

The day Ruth drove her husband to the airport for his European trip, she said, "How many fireplaces can I have?"

"No more than two," Mr. Graham said.

Upon his return, he found a beautiful home with five fireplaces. Ruth said, "I thought you said no *fewer* than two."

When recounting this story for me, she winked and said, "There comes a time to stop submitting and start outwitting."

Those fireplaces are part of the glory of that home, and in his age and infirmity, Mr. Graham loves them all—as I assume his wife knew he would.

At another point in our interviews, Mr. Graham related a story about how his first fiancée dumped him, long before he had met Ruth. While he was in the middle of the tale, Ruth marched in and plopped down a big box of tissues next to him. He squinted. "Did I ask for these?"

"No," she said, "but you sound like you need them."

One day, while conducting our interviews in the library of his modest office, he told his secretary to hold his calls. I had both of us wired up with lapel microphones, and we were poring over boxes of keepsakes and records.

About twenty minutes later, his secretary interrupted and whispered, "There is a call you'll want to take." I assumed it was personal, from Ruth or one of their five kids.

I helped extricate him from the mike clip, and while he was away, I decided I'd make a stab at humor when he returned. When he came back in, I said, "So, what did the President want?"

He blanched. "Well, I'm not at liberty to say." And he glanced at his secretary in obvious disappointment that she would share such a confidence.

"Oh, she didn't say anything," I said. "I was just joking."

Yeah. Hilarious.

One of the more interesting things I learned while working with Mr. Graham is that he believes he preaches the most misunderstood message ever.

"In what way?" I said.

"I've been preaching for more than fifty years," he said. "I've spoken on radio and television and in stadiums all over the world, and I always say the same thing. Yet you ask the common man on the street what I say is the way to heaven, and nine of ten will say, you need to live a good life, follow the Golden Rule, make positive choices, go to church, be nice to people, and do the right things. But I've never preached that. I preach the opposite.

"People are to try to live right, of course, but not as a way to earn heaven, because they could never do enough. They should live right in gratitude to God for His gift of salvation through His Son. The Bible says there is 'none righteous, no not one.'"

While we were working together in Florida, Mr. Graham was getting a haircut in the hotel barbershop. The manicurist, seemingly just to make conversation, said, "So what do you do?"

In his inimitable voice and accent, Mr. Graham said, "I'm a preachah."

"Oh, you're a preacher," she said. "I don't care too much for preachers. In fact, the only one I listen to is Billy Graham."

"You like Billy Graham, do you?"

"Oh, yes. I watch him on television and love to hear him."

"Well, thank you. I am Billy Graham."

"Oh," she said, laughing, "you don't even look like him."

The barber mouthed to her from behind Mr. Graham, "It's really him."

"Oh, my God," she said.

"No," Mr. Graham said, "but I work for Him."

One Sunday morning, we attended church near his home. Even there his presence causes a stir, so we slipped in late to avoid a scene. During the song service, I shared a hymnbook with him. *Here I am*, I thought, *singing with Billy Graham*. But that so overwhelmed me that I choked up and couldn't sing. Mr. Graham can't carry a tune. He seems to have only one note, and it doesn't match anything on the musical scale. So there we were, I too overcome to sing and he growling out his one note. But we were sharing that hymnbook.

Late in the interviewing process, I realized I had tons of material, but worried I didn't have a lot of the all-important take-away value for the reader. It's one thing to chronicle the life of one of the religious luminaries of the twentieth century, but quite another to leave the reader with something of value to his own life.

Besides being a larger-than-life personality, to people of faith Mr. Graham has long been an icon, an example. While many so-called Christian leaders have been exposed in all their frailty and egocentricities, Billy Graham has been a model of consistency and humility. Even those who disagree with his message acknowledge that he is a man of God who walks the walk.

I wanted to leave the reader with nuggets of wisdom from this man, who seems to have his spiritual life in order, but I went about asking for them entirely the wrong way. I said that many people, especially evangelicals, see him as the epitome of the consistent Christian life. Before I could even get to my question of how he does it, he began to wave me off.

"Oh, they mustn't," he said.

More of that humility, I decided.

"Maybe they shouldn't," I said, "but they put you on a pedestal as a model of spirituality, and—"

He was still waving me off. "No, they really shouldn't. When I think of the number of times I've failed the Lord, I feel this low." And he leaned over the side of his chair and pressed his palm flat on the floor.

Now this was too much. Billy Graham? The man who has spoken to more people in live audiences than anyone else in history? The man who has spent nearly his entire life pointing people to God? The man whose life and ministry has been under press scrutiny for nearly sixty years and who has always emerged squeaky clean?

I said, "But you're seen as almost the Protestant Pope. Surely there are secrets, hints you can offer laypeople on how to maintain their walk with God...."

"They shouldn't look to me."

"But they do."

He wouldn't budge, but finally I hit upon the approach that worked. "Tell me, at least, how you maintain your own spiritual disciplines."

His eyes lit up. "There's no secret to that," he said. "God doesn't hide the key from us. The Bible says to pray without ceasing and to search the Scriptures. And I do that."

I flinched. I had always hoped the Apostle Paul's New Testament admonition to "pray without ceasing" was somehow figurative. After two to three minutes of prayer, my mind tends to wander, and I find myself wondering whether the Cubs will ever see another World Series. (Talk about a miracle.)

"You pray without ceasing?" I said.

"I do," Mr. Graham said, still with that air of pure humility. "And I have, every waking moment since I received Christ as a teenager." He had to have seen the doubt on my face. "I'm praying right now as I'm talking to you," he said. "Praying that God will use this book, that it will be clear that it's more about Him than about me, praying that we'll both do our jobs well and that He will get the glory."

I was nearly speechless. "And your searching the Scripture," I managed, "how does that work?"

"Wherever I am," he said, "at home, in my office, or in a hotel room in some other country, the first thing I do in the morning is to leave my Bible open somewhere where I will notice it during the day. I pick it up at odd moments and read a verse or two or a chapter or two or for an hour or two. And this is not for study or sermon preparation. This is just for my own spiritual nourishment."

Now we were getting somewhere. Everyone I know who is serious about his spiritual life would love to have a more consistent devotional life of prayer and Bible reading. Perhaps I was on the edge of real takeaway value.

"Say you miss a day or two," I said. "How do you get back to your routine?"

"Miss a day or two?" he said. "I don't think I've ever done that."

"You never miss?"

He shook his head. "I told you. This is my spiritual food. I would no more miss this than a regular meal."

I went back to my hotel that day despairing that perhaps no reader could really identify with a man so sold out to God and so disciplined in his inner life. But then it hit me. As he said, it's no secret, no hidden key—God doesn't make it hard or a mystery. When people wonder why Billy Graham, among all those claiming the same passions, seems infinitely more blessed, more successful (for lack of a better term) in his ministry efforts, they need to realize there is a difference between him and the others: We all know we're to pray and read our Bibles. The difference is, he does it.

I had not seen Mr. Graham for several years when I hosted our Christian Writers Guild Writing for the Soul conference at his training center, The Cove, in Asheville, North Carolina, in August of 2003. What a privilege to get a few minutes with him. Though by then he was well into his eighties and his health was clearly failing, he proved well read, up-to-date on current events and politics, and he also said the most poignant thing.

He and Ruth were coming up on their sixtieth wedding anniversary, but she could not join us for lunch because her health was even more frail than his. "We have learned, however," he said, "that even at this stage of life, we can continue our love affair with our eyes."

By the same time the following year, Mr. Graham and Ruth were confined to their home with various ailments. Dianna and

I found him in bed with a broken pelvis. Regardless, he looked majestic, with those piercing blue eyes and that mane of white hair. He told us that his doctor had come the day before to give him an injection directly into the pelvic bone, and that the man had warned him it would be very painful.

"The doctor told me to imagine the one place I'd rather be than this, a Shangri-la of some sort, and concentrate on that. I told him, 'There's nowhere I'd rather be than right here, right now.' The doctor said, 'Why in the world would you say that? I told you, this is really going to hurt.'

"I told him, 'Because I believe I'm in the center of God's will, and if this is where He wants me, this is where I want to be.'"

There's a lesson for everybody, especially inspirational writers.

CHAPTER
5

What to Write

Early in my writing career, I'd accept just about any assignment. I'd hop from a nonfiction project to a first-person, as-told-to story. Then I'd write a marriage and family title, then children's fiction, then adult. When asked what was my favorite, I would say, "Whatever I'm not doing right now."

I didn't want to write the same thing all the time, unless I could write only adult mainstream fiction. And, as I have said, you can't do that unless you have a hit, or you'll starve. I enjoyed trying everything.

But I had a hit in *Left Behind*, and with it came the freedom to write what I wanted. I've narrowed that primarily to fiction for adults, but variety still keeps the batteries fresh. The desire to try something different inspired *Though None Go With Me*, *'Twas the Night Before*, *The Youngest Hero*, and, most recently, *Holding Heaven*. I'll always be identified with futuristic apocalyptic fiction, but I wouldn't want to be locked into solely that. The titles above represent historical fiction, fantasy, mainstream fiction, and the geopolitical thriller.

I urge you to test all the waters that interest you. Discover where your strengths lie. Then inject who you are into your writing.

WHERE TO BEGIN

Beginning writers are told to write what they know. Now may be the season of life to write your family history, keep up with correspondence, or pen poetry. You might enjoy creating a family newsletter or keeping your home Web page updated. Those are worthy goals. I've helped my mother put together anthologies of my father's poetry and publish them for our family and friends. These are treasures. I also wrote and published a history of my hundred-year-old grandmother-in-law.

I did these projects as labors of love after I was a widely published author, but it strikes me that such projects—and many other types— would have been ideal for someone just starting out. You want to be a writer, people tell you that you have a knack, but how do you break in? And before that great day comes when you actually sell a piece of your work, how do you do the work of a writer? By writing.

Does your church have a newsletter? You can bet that whoever is putting it together would love to have more material to work with. Interview anyone in your church with an interesting history or story. Your byline appearing in print will be your only pay, but you will be exercising muscles you'll need in your writing career.

Is there a community flyer that circulates in your neighborhood, or a free paper that is mostly advertising? Many of these contain fillers and general-interest articles their publishers get free from various sources. Find out who publishes that flyer and see if that publisher would like some local news to really make it sing. Again, you may be donating your time and work, but you *are* getting started.

Do you belong to a group, organization, or club that needs a newsletter? Volunteer to handle it; write all the pieces yourself. Someday you may look back and fret over how amateurish the writing seems, and you may wish you'd had an editor. But you will have gained invaluable experience nonetheless.

Most of the published writers I know have some background in journalism. If you're having trouble starting, or breaking into print, you might want to find an evening course and study newspaper writing, news reporting, or feature writing. One quarter or semester could unlock a door for you. I studied journalism in high school and college, and worked in the field for many years.

Journalism teaches you to get to the point and write quickly. You also learn to write regardless of the distractions. Some need solitude to focus and write. I find that to be the case when I'm working on a book, because, while I have never been diagnosed with ADD, I do find myself unendingly curious about mail, visitors, phone calls, e-mail, what's on the radio or TV. I need to get away to what I call my cave to have any hope of making my deadlines. But when it comes to newspaper or magazine writing, strangely, it's the opposite. I seemed to be able to write even with activity all around me. I believe that's because of my roots in journalism.

When I started in the newspaper business, I worked in a large room filled with islands consisting of four metal desks shoved together. Everyone worked against a backdrop of clacking typewriters,[1] tinny Teletype machines, and ringing phones. People walked about, talking and laughing; they sometimes wrestled, and often even threw things. (We invented games involving crumpled up paper and wastebaskets; don't ask.)

---

[1] Recently, while speaking to a group of college kids, I mentioned starting my career on a manual typewriter, and, thinking I was being funny, I said, "I'm sure some of you have heard of the typewriter." A girl raised her hand and exulted, "I think I actually saw one once!"

Often, anybody not writing was playing that game or tossing around a Nerf football. The closer it came to deadline time, the fewer the people who played and gabbed and the more frantic the writing pace. In a strange way, it was great fun. That's how we worked. We had no choice.

Occasionally somebody who had just graduated from journalism school (J-schoolers, we called 'em) would holler, "Could you please be quiet? I'm writing!" We'd laugh and throw things at them, where-upon they would complain to the big boss—who would also laugh and throw things.

Listen, it helps to learn to write in a boiler-room atmosphere. Do that and you can write anywhere.

WHAT NOT TO WRITE

One of the most common mistakes new writers make is trying to start their career with a book. That's like starting your education in graduate school. Start small. Write for the joy of it, to see your name in print, even if you're giving your work away or being paid in copies. You need to work countless clichés out of your system, tone writing muscles, and learn both the business and the craft.

I always encourage writers to approach magazines and newspapers and get experience writing articles before tackling their novels. See what your stuff looks like in print, and be your own toughest critic.

Learn everything there is to know about how to submit your material, then start small. Write for local publications, and when you have scored some clips, try regional magazines, then national. You'll stub your toe occasionally, but you'll learn. You'd be surprised at how many submissions magazine editors get from people who don't even know to double-space their work and print it on only one side of the paper.

An even larger issue is trying to write on issues beyond your grasp as a beginner—writing a memoir when you're only in your twenties, for instance. While your story may be huge and significant, you'll need years of mature reflection before you can make sense of it and present it so it will have a real impact on readers. Even if you're a mature thinker already, are you far enough along with your writing skills to do justice to the topic?

I have been a church-going Christian all my life, and attended Bible college right out of high school, but even today I wouldn't dream of trying to tackle theological and biblical subjects on my own. If Dr. Tim LaHaye can be honest and self-aware enough to admit that—despite his many considerable gifts and abilities—he's not a fiction writer, I must concede that I'm no scholar or theologian.

As a magazine editor, I once received a letter from a teenager querying me on a 1,500-word, first-person piece entitled "The Meaning of the Universe." Attempting such a project is akin to my trying to write a brief essay that would solve the conflict in Northern Ireland. There may well be those with experience and expertise and legitimate insight into that, but I'm not one of them. We write to learn, but let's remember that a little knowledge can be dangerous. Either make thorough use of interviews with experts in the area you wish to write about, or stick to what you really know.

FINDING IDEAS

Let's say you've published widely in magazines or newspapers, and you want to try your hand at a novel. People often ask me, "Where do your ideas come from?" Everywhere. But usually they begin as unusual combinations. A woman whose life mirrors that of Job. The end of the world if played out as it seems to be prophesied in the Bible. The youngest big league baseball player in history.

That last idea came to me when my eldest son, Dallas—then eleven years old—and I were playing catch in the yard, and I was lofting high, arcing tosses that made him run to chase down the ball. As kids often do, he was shouting a running play-by-play. "Dallas Jenkins races back to the wall to make the catch! The youngest player in the history of the Chicago Cubs fires the ball back into the infield...."

And it hit me. He didn't want to be a big-leaguer when he grew up; he wanted to be a big-leaguer right then! That rattled around in my brain for several weeks, until I began wondering how young a player might be and still actually make the big leagues. (The record was set during World War II by Joe Nuxhall, who, at fifteen, was built like a man. Joe pitched during the war, when many of the pros were in the military.)

I didn't want to write a fantasy in which a kid gets a bionic appendage. I wanted to write a story as if it could really happen: A bigger-, smarter-, faster-than-average kid has the right genes (his father was a minor league star), and circumstances converge to make him a prodigy. That idea became the book *Rookie*, which is now published under the title *The Youngest Hero*.

Would-be writers often read a book and decide they could have done better. That's a start. Don't criticize. Don't complain. Don't talk about what you would have done differently; do it. Start with your own characters, and come up with something fresh and believable. If you think you can write better than the bestsellers, who's to say you can't?

As I've said, all the big names were beginners once. Editors are looking for writers, regardless of whether they've been published before. Yes, the competition is fiercer than it's ever been, and yes, someone with an already-established name has an edge. But more than anything, an editor wants to say, "I've discovered the next talent."

Here are a few ways to come up with your own fresh and believable stories.

NEWSPAPER

It's hard to beat the newspaper as a source for story ideas. You'd be amazed at how mixing and matching works here. Start with a tragic story from the front page, then find a trivial local piece on an inside page. Imagine a normal person from the local story thrust into the big story. How would that happen? Is she on vacation for her twenty-fifth service anniversary, enjoying her first time out of the country, when a hurricane hits her resort? Then what happens? Does Ms. Milquetoast, hardly a blip on anyone's radar, discover heroic tendencies that make her a rescuer?

I like to put normal people in unusual situations. Other novelists prefer chronicling the lives of the rich and powerful and famous. Stir the stew however you like, and see how it tastes at the keyboard.

THE THEATER OF YOUR OWN MIND

Here's an exercise that might help. Imagine two dirt roads crossing in the middle of nowhere. No noise, no traffic. Smell the dry, dark dirt, feel the sun.

Far in the distance, you see a cloud of dust, and gradually a shimmering vehicle comes into view. As it draws nearer, you see it's a Greyhound bus. It stops at the crossroad, and a person emerges. The bus pulls away.

Now tell me:

- Is the person who got off the bus a man, a woman, a child? White, Black, Hispanic, Asian, Middle Eastern, some other ethnicity?
- What does the person look like?
- How is she dressed?
- Is she alone?
- Is anyone waiting for her?
- What is she carrying?

Trust me, if you continue this line of thinking, a story will wash over you. Where is this person coming from and where is she going? Who will she see next? What will happen? What's the trouble? What needs to happen? What's at stake?

My story would be wholly different from yours. I might imagine a young, pregnant woman who had scraped together just enough money to escape an abusive husband and ride from the South to the West to take refuge with her sister. She's not even carrying a suitcase, and her shoes are not appropriate for the season or the place.

You might imagine an old Eastern European man, laden with a trunk, looking for someone. Who? A long-lost friend? A long-lost love? A loved one who recently went missing?

Keep asking questions. If the answer doesn't come, sleep on it. You may wake up eager to get to the keyboard.

If you get stuck, leave that lonely character in the wilds and see who gets off the bus at the next stop. And where is that? And who is that?

AUTOBIOGRAPHICAL FICTION

Most novelists draw from their own experience. We have to. I must put myself in the place of each of my characters: old, young, male, female, hero, villain, or utility character. I imagine myself as that person and decide how I would react and what I would say in every situation. My mother has said that she sees me in every character.

A caution: When writing about something wholly apart from your own experience, you'll want to do some thorough research first. I can *imagine* myself as the other gender, *imagine* how it would feel, say, to lose a child, *imagine* becoming so vengeful that I might want to kill someone. But if I were going to write about a mother who lost a child due to someone's carelessness or negligence or—worse—spite, I'd be wise to interview a woman who has endured such a tragedy.

I've seen countless movies and TV shows portraying homicide detectives. My father was a cop, and my two older brothers became cops. I've probably been exposed to more police stations and law enforcement officers than the average person. But I wouldn't dare try to write a serious novel about homicide detectives without doing some real homework: ride-alongs with real detectives, interviews, watching the detectives work.

Now, when I write about my detective character approaching a locked apartment, not knowing whether someone on the other side could fire a shotgun blast through the door, I'll imagine my fear in the same situation. How the character handles that situation, however, will come from careful research.

Most of the scenarios in the Left Behind series are imagined, of course. I haven't lived through the Rapture, but I have been scared to death. I haven't lived through a war, but I was thirty blocks north of the World Trade Center when it was attacked. My imagination must fill in the blanks.

What would it be like to live through the aftermath of the Rapture, during the seven years of Tribulation? What if I were a new mother during this time? Would I consider killing my own child rather than have her fall into the hands of the enemy? How could a mother even think such a thing?

Citizens of Masada faced exactly that decision in 73 A.D. They killed their offspring and themselves rather than fall under the power of the enemy. To them, there was nothing worse than having their kids brainwashed, their beliefs obliterated.

That's another reason to be a reading writer: History can help you make believable plotting decisions. It puts you in times and places centuries before you were born and makes you imagine what you might have done in the same situations. You cannot write credible characters otherwise.

AWAY FROM HOME

Keep your antenna up whenever you're away from home, even when you're just at the mall or visiting an unfamiliar street in your area. Jump at any opportunity to travel to other states or countries, keep eyes and ears open, and learn as you go. You never know what stored tidbit will find its way onto your pages.

Be aware of your surroundings at:

- the grocery store
- a museum
- an art gallery
- the zoo
- the office

Regardless of where you work, you have access to a cast of unique characters. Do you work in an office? A corporation? You could probably script a soap opera.

Don't let the daily grind go to waste. Find the germs for stories in the mundane, but mix in something extra, that what-if factor. I just heard a bizarre story of a man who accidentally bumped his cell phone, calling his wife. His phone reached her answering machine, and when he then called his mistress, the calls were conferenced. That sounds like a bad movie, doesn't it? But doesn't it also spark an idea? Can you come up with a similar comedy of errors that becomes tragic?

You're limited only by your personal creativity and your ability to connect disparate events and characters to create grist for a story. Maybe a character has been playing at the edges of your consciousness for a while. Pin her outline on your mechanic or your dentist and start playing what-if. It's how novelists think.

B.J. THOMAS

My mother is a musician and has been a piano student and teacher for most of her life. She was a soloist and choir director at our church during my growing-up years. I've always loved singing and music, though I never learned an instrument, so it has been fun to be involved with musicians in writing their books. I've worked with Christian artist Christine Wyrtzen, Southern Gospel aficionado and composer Bill Gaither, and pop superstar B.J. Thomas.

As a lover of words, I have always been most moved by song lyrics. Much can be learned from songwriters, who are true poets, putting as much emphasis and meaning as possible into the fewest possible words, and evoking emotion while doing so.

B.J. Thomas, most famous for making a mega-hit of Burt Bacharach's "Raindrops Keep Fallin' on My Head" in 1969, has a unique sound and a powerful story of love and redemption, kicking drugs, coming to faith, and navigating a tumultuous career. What fun it was to be exposed to that world, joining him backstage in Las Vegas, watching from the wings as he performed, and—best of all—enjoying the recording studio experience.

One night in Memphis, as he was working hard on "Every-body Loves a Rain Song" for producer and writer Chips Mo-man—who was running the board in the control room—B.J. just nailed a perfect take. I had become fascinated watching Mo-man, his fingers flying over the controls while he smiled broadly as B.J. neared the end. It was as if Chips was praying B.J. could finish as strongly as he had begun.

B.J. seemed to know he had scored when he hit the final note and he looked through the glass for Chips's approval. Chips leaped from his chair, fists in the air, and exulted, "Put the chairs on the wagon, the meetin's over!"

It was a moment, and a phrase, I'll never forget.

CHAPTER
6

Equipping Your Writing Space

Many novelists write every day; I write only on deadline. It's always been that way, and I seem to be more productive with that approach. Once my research is done and I'm ready to hunker down, I figure how many days it will take to make my deadline, writing a certain number of pages per day. Then I go off and do only that. If I fall behind, I increase the number of pages I must produce each day. While I am ferocious about making the deadline, my top priority is submitting my best work. If I need an extension, I ask for it. I won't submit anything I'm not entirely happy with.

When it's time to get down to writing, I head to my writing retreat in the mountains, which sits on the second floor of a building behind a large cabin home on fifty-nine acres. But even when my sanctuary consisted of only a cheap hotel room or my own basement, I always referred to my writing space as my cave, because it was simple and bereft of distractions.

One key to successful writing is having a place dedicated solely to that purpose. When I was starting out, of course, we lived in a tiny house with no garage and certainly no work space for an author. I had started with an old upright manual typewriter, pecking away with two fingers. My ersatz office consisted of the couch, where I sat with my new portable electric typewriter facing me on the seat of a kitchen chair. I spread my papers on either side of me, and if I had a lot of resources to consult, I added a kitchen chair on either side of the typewriter.

When we moved into a bigger house and I was able to dedicate a room (or a corner in the cellar) to my writing, I set up a cockpit, with my computer next to the printer, phone and fax machine in easy reach, and a tape recorder for phone interviews. I kept everything close and used a rolling cart for stuff I needed only some of the time. I also had a television in case of big news, but I denied myself a remote control. I had to walk over to turn on the TV or switch channels. (With a remote control I could have easily switched to ball games and gotten little else done.)

Eventually I found I needed a space outside the house. Sometimes I checked into an inexpensive extended-stay hotel. Quickly tiring of being away from my wife, I fashioned a writing lair above the garage. Then I built an office building next door, only to find that while I could *work* there, I couldn't *write* there. I don't know about you, but I must be away from visitors, the mail, and the phone, because I'm incorrigibly curious and have a doctorate in procrastination.

It might comfort you to know that I have come to believe that pro-crastination is not just a necessary evil, it's a prerequisite to the writing process. Seriously, you are in the minority if you are a writer but not a procrastinator. If you're like me, however, you must learn to manage procrastination rather than stress over it. I used to lose sleep as poten-tially productive days slipped past with nothing to show for them. I now realize that all during that time—when I am consumed, for no logical reason, with tidying my office or restocking my supplies or reading every word of every aged magazine in my pile—my subconscious is working on the story, and once I start writing, it will come.

Writing is like a long run to a place I've never been. I'm eager and can't wait to get started, yet I put it off because I know it's going to be grueling and will take longer than I imagine. The destination will ultimately be satisfying, but getting there will be an ordeal.

The difference between my procrastination and that of others? I consider deadlines sacrosanct. I may put off the work, but I always leave time to make that deadline.

Now, because I have businesses and employees, it's even more important that I get away to write. And the farther away, the better. Admittedly, my place in the mountains is a pretty nice cave, but I still call it that because it is simple. I have my resources, my research, and the best equipment I can afford: computer, monitor, printer, etc. And although I have pictures on the wall and books on the shelves, nothing else intrudes. No phone, no Internet, no radio, no TV, no video or computer games. That's why a writing cave is so crucial. There I can only write or procrastinate, and often I do a good deal of both.

My cave, with its panoramic views of mountain peaks and buffalo-dotted plains, is a retreat for the eyes and mind. Such an idyllic setting leaves me wholly without excuse for not getting my work done. Inspiration lies just outside the windows on three walls. I get plenty of light, sometimes too much. Depending on the time of day, I pull the shades on one side or another to avoid glare.

Next to the cave is a bathroom, and down the hall is a workout room. Being a morning person, I can rise, have breakfast, dress in workout clothes (carrying my writing clothes), head to the cave, work out, shower, change, and get to work. With a mini-fridge stocked with water and Diet Coke, I can settle in until lunchtime, then again until my work is done or dinnertime, whichever comes first. I don't leave the cave for the day until my pages are done.

THE RIGHT EQUIPMENT FOR THE JOB

Regardless where you are on your writing journey, strive for the best space and the best equipment you can afford. Believe me, you'll appreciate the difference.

I worked construction after high school to pay for my first year of college. One day, my foreman had trouble removing a manhole cover, so he brought in a massive forklift truck designed to deliver huge pallets of supplies to the home sites. He looped a chain through the holes in the cover and wrapped it around one of the forks.

He signaled the operator to raise the forks, which quickly eliminated the slack. The machine strained at the cover. I found a safe place to watch, because the chain links seemed to actually stretch. I could imagine one becoming a deadly weapon if the chain snapped.

Fortunately, the manhole cover gave way before the chain did, but then it itself became a missile. It flew straight up about thirty feet, flipping like Paul Bunyan's quarter, then landed on its edge, lodging halfway into the asphalt.

My boss's boss had happened by when the show began, and he gave us his profane assessment of the witless foreman. "You used too much tool for the job!" My boss had endangered lives and wasted resources.

As your career grows, you may find yourself lusting after every gadget that promises to make your work easier. While I advise saving your money for what you really need, having too little equipment for the job is as bad as having too much. It'll take some trial and error, but eventually you'll learn what is essential.

If you have to stretch or even go into debt for any one thing, it should be your chair. You are going to live in that thing for hours at a time, and you want to be able to forget about it. How can you concentrate on the myriad elements of a piece of writing if you're worried about your back or your neck or your eyes? You'll regret buying the wrong chair, and you and your writing will suffer. Worse, you'll come to dread your time at the keyboard.

Fortunately, computers have become economical enough for almost anyone, and you can easily skip the bells and whistles that run up the price. Go for speed and disk space, and, of course, word-processing software compatible with most publishers. That generally means Microsoft Word on a Windows machine or a Mac.

I remove the games that come with new machines, because I don't need one more distracting temptation. Have you ever promised yourself a game of Minesweeper or solitaire upon finishing a chapter and then wasted several hours with "just one more"? Yeah, neither have I.

I bought my first IBM Correcting Selectric typewriter for a whopping $650 back in the 1970s. I felt so guilty. How could I ever justify spending that much? But it made mistakes magically disappear. Only a few years later I took out a bank loan to invest in an IBM Memory Typewriter (essentially a magnetic-tape-driven word processor, minus the screen). Talk about magic.

Finally, I moved to a word-processing computer. That first computer, way back in 1980, was an all-in-one unit that used five-and-a-quarter-inch floppies that were really floppy. I had to pull the WordStar disk from the slot and replace it with my spell-checking software. But to be able to check the spelling of an entire file in just a matter of minutes? I couldn't imagine anything so quick. Nowadays, if my computer hesitates a nanosecond, I'm grumbling, "Come onnnnnnn!"

Benefits

When my cave was a hotel room, my time away from Dianna was far less productive because it was so lonely. Nowadays, when I'm in the cave, she's a hundred feet away in the house, and we're together for meals and when I'm done each day. She is my reward for finishing. Plus, I love talking about scenes with her before I commit them to the page. Most novelists fear losing their creativity if they utter even a word of the story before getting it on paper. But every time I tell a story, I embellish it. Characterizations flesh out, the plot grows. I hone the details and get instant feedback about whether I'll be able to keep the attention of my reader.

Ideas tend to come easier when your writing space and tools are right. Yet ideas for scenes and stories seem to hit me most often in the shower. Maybe the shooting streams of water stimulate my brain. Or maybe it's because I can relax alone and think.

Words come slower to me at the keyboard some days, but I learned years ago to trust what some call the Muse. My muse is spiritual, a vital part of the creative subconscious I have surrendered to God. Foreshadowing and plot threads appear as I write. I may not be sure at the time why I include certain things, but later in the manuscript, the reasons become obvious. Loose ends come together.

I know there are exceptions to these guidelines about equipment, and sometimes they are visible ones—like veteran bestsellers still writing by hand or manual typewriter—but trust me, today it's naive for a freelance writer to think he can get along without a computer or Internet access. It won't be long before writing any other way will sound like using a quill and ink.

Get over your love affair with the old methods, and turn your typewriter into a conversation piece. If it's true that only one in a thousand freelancers gets published, assume that your competition is already computer literate and has access to computer-assisted research.

You can deduct every dime of all these expenses if you make sure everything is used only for your writing. That gives you the right to keep the rest of the family off your computer. And if you dedicate a room of your house solely to your office, you can write off to your business a percentage of your utilities and even some of your rent or mortgage.

RECHARGING THE BATTERIES

I'm often asked what it's like to be a full-time freelancer, as if the glamour outweighs all. I say, "You want the truth? It's like having homework every day for the rest of your life." There comes a time when you have to get completely away from writing.

Anything other than writing I consider downtime. Traveling, speaking, media appearances, my businesses, you name it—if I'm not writing, I feel as if I'm enjoying time off. There's still pressure and tension and challenge in many of the things that occupy me, but nothing saps my energy like writing.

Although many activities feel like downtime while I'm writing, I have to take a real vacation right after a deadline. Between one deadline and the start of the next project, I need crash time, a week or two to get away and do nothing: talking, sitting by a pool and reading, the only decision being where Dianna and I will have dinner each night.

Q & A WITH JERRY

You're an extremely fast writer. Do I have to write fast to succeed?

No. If you write quickly and your writing looks dashed off, you'll regret it. Although I write fast (because, I think, of my journalism training), I never want my finished product to appear rushed. I care about every word and want that to show. At a certain point, however, reworking something makes it only different, not better.

I have friends who struggle over every page. Sometimes they labor for hours on a single paragraph. That doesn't make them slow writers. They simply take more time up front; my tedious work comes at the other end of the process. I get that first draft down and see it as a hunk of meat to be carved. You have to find what works best for you and stick with that.

How do you avoid distractions?

Only by cutting them out in advance, as in erasing the games off my computer and not having radio, TV, phone, or Internet in my cave. Still, it's hard for me to concentrate on one thing. I'd rather start something than finish. I'd rather dream up something new. I find planning more fun than doing. But as an author, I don't have that luxury. Once committed, I must finish, and on time. Writing in seclusion helps.

Is there any excuse for saying "I won't write today?"

Sometimes. If you're under the weather or didn't sleep well, maybe you need a break. Maybe your creative juices will flow better if you give yourself a day off. But you always have to pay.

I can sometimes talk myself out of writing for a day by telling myself I'm starting too late and not going to get enough done anyway. I blow off the day and plan to start early the next. That gives a sense of real, though temporary, freedom. I'll ride along with Dianna while she shops, sit in the car reading a novel, work a crossword puzzle, enjoy a meal. I'll think that maybe I needed the day off. Maybe I deserved it.

But the next day I have to write twice as long, and that's the price. It's exhausting, but we reap what we sow. Better to stay disciplined and get your pages done every day, working through a little illness or fatigue. Then you can take breaks.

Is there a time of day when you write best?

First thing in the morning. In the morning, I haven't allowed anything else to cloud my mind. I can concentrate. What I write before noon is always my best work, and the most work I'll complete all day.

I always start by editing the previous day's pages. Then my goal is to write half my allotted pages before lunchtime. If I start early and things go well, I can occasionally get all my pages for the day done before noon. Some might then try to knock out another batch to make the next day easier. Not me. That's it for the day. But if it takes till midnight to finish my pages, I do it. I don't want to fall behind and be forced to write more the next day.

Whether you are a morning person or a night person or both, it's best to write when you feel fully rested and awake. But how many people ever feel that way? If you get tired, take a nap. But if you're waiting until you're completely cogent, coherent, and inspired, you may never get to the keyboard. You become a better writer by writing, by flexing those writing muscles.

How can a freelancer get organized enough to work at home?

A stay-at-home parent probably won't get much freelancing done until the kids are in school. Nothing's tougher than keeping a home and family together. Some can do it while writing, but it's nearly impossible.

However, if you're actually being published, you're probably making more per hour writing than you'd ever pay somebody to help clean your house or run errands. If so, hire some help and write.

Another option is to give yourself a set period, maybe two years, to become a self-sustaining writer. If it doesn't work, try something else.

Did that last sentence resonate with you? If it did, you're not cut out to be a writer. A writer would say, "If it doesn't work, I'll wait till the kids are older, but I'm not giving up."

MEADOWLARK LEMON

I first saw the Harlem Globetrotters when I was in sixth grade, and they were all I could talk about for days. My brothers and my friends and I loved the main clown, Meadowlark Lemon. To write his book years later was a thrill.

Of all the sports stars I wrote about, only a few actually visited my house. Usually I went to them. But Meadowlark dropped in on me while traveling through Chicago. In this one instance, I had to violate my policy to never ask my subjects for anything but their time. I told him, "I hate to ask, but I'd never forgive myself if I didn't have you shoot a basket through my hoop."

He was glad to do it, so we went out to the driveway where my boys and I had played so many times. We lived in the country, and our driveway was about a hundred feet long, curving past some trees. Meadowlark warmed up by shooting a few baskets from close range, then started dribbling away from the basket, moving about fifty feet down the driveway and behind the trees.

He had a patented half-court hook shot that had thrilled audiences around the world for years. Was he about to try that from an even longer range? I said, "I need to tell you, our basket is only nine-foot-six." (My kids were still little. Regulation rim height is ten feet.)

Meadowlark said, "I can see how high your basket is. I played in seventy-five hundred straight games."

He peeked around the trees for reference, then dribbled twice and launched a high-arcing hook shot. While it was in the air, he shouted, "If it gets anything but net, I don't want it!"

I wish I'd gotten that on video. Nothing but net.

Later, he wanted to work out indoors with a regulation hoop, so I took him to a local school and offered to rebound for him. I stood under the basket, grabbing the ball as it came through the basket and firing passes to him all over the court. I couldn't believe it. I stood in one spot for more than ten minutes, because no matter where he shot from, regardless of whether the ball banked off the backboard, swished, or rattled through, he didn't miss a shot. That ball dropped at my feet every time, and I barely had to reach for it, and never had to take a step. All I had to do was gather it in and pass it back to him. Yet he played so effortlessly that it seemed I was working harder than he was.

One of the great memories of that project was traveling with Meadowlark to his hometown, Wilmington, North Carolina. By the time I worked with him, his glory days were over, but that was certainly not the case in Wilmington. He was treated like a god.

He had told no one he was coming, but word spread fast as we drove and walked around town, visiting his favorite childhood haunts: the local movie theater where he had seen a Globetrotter documentary as a child, his school, his church, his home.

People began gathering, surrounding him, shaking hands, following, remembering. The local boys' club that had been so instrumental in his development as a child (and which now bore his name) became a gathering place for several of his high school teammates from more than forty years before. I just kept a tape recorder rolling as they joked and laughed and reminisced. What a treasure of stories!

Most fun was when they began to play what they called "the dozens." No one could tell me where the name came from, but it was basically these guys trying to top each other with creative insults.

"You're gettin' so fat you're gonna need your own zip code!"

"You're so stupid, you heard it was chilly outside, you went and got a spoon."

All these were said with such good humor that the friends howled till they cried, rocking and holding their stomachs.

We met with some of Meadowlark's teachers, his high school coach, and many of his relatives. To this day, I believe Meadowlark considered that visit the highlight of the entire book project.

CHAPTER
7

Writers Are Readers

I was raised by a crossword-puzzling, poetic father and an anagramming, word-loving, Latin-knowing, grammarian mother. My two older brothers are smart and were good students, so I learned to speak and write correctly by osmosis, which frustrated my English teachers to no end. I could pick out the correct sentence, but I couldn't say why it was better than the poor example—it just sounded right. The right one sounded the way my mother spoke.

I learned to read before kindergarten, and in those days learning to read wasn't supposed to happen until first grade. I'd have gone stir crazy waiting that long, so I read to my kindergarten colleagues and got a reputation for being smart. My friends even asked me if Santa was real, as if, because I could read, I must know. Of course I knew, and I assured them he was and believed it from the core of my being. (More than forty years later I wrote *'Twas the Night Before*, a novel that proved me right.)

From early reading came a love for newspapers and magazines—something fresh and new to read every day! And from all that reading, I think, came an ear or an eye for good writing. I was great in arithmetic until it became geometry and algebra, and I was good in science until it became biology and chemistry. But give me a writing assignment, and I was in heaven. That I could do. The fact that most kids loved all that other stuff but dreaded writing made me somewhat unique.

Writers must love words. That's a prerequisite. I especially love anagrams, interesting turns of phrase, mistakes, typographical errors, unintentionally funny signs (Discount Foods & Salvage), and the like.

I drive family and friends crazy when I see an interesting word and notice it's an anagram for something else (an anagram is a word formed from the same letters as another word). For instance, I'll drive past a car and call out, "Anagram for *Pontiac!*" A lover of words will soon come up with *caption.* Or we'll pull into a hotel and I'll say, "Anagram for *Hampton.*" *Phantom.*

My mother and my brothers and I like to e-mail each other interesting word play and stories—like the story of the woman who told my brother he was "*grammarically* correct." Someone once sent me an e-mail that said, "Don't worry about dumb people, because *there* stupid." They certainly are. I once heard a horticulturalist say, "You can say herb or 'erb; either *pronounciation* is correct."

I also love beautiful writing. Writers are readers. Good writers are good readers. Great writers are great readers. If you don't like to read, you may want to consider another profession. So much of our art is learned by osmosis.

I read some writers and strive to be like them. I read others, like Rick Bragg, the Pulitzer Prize–winning former *New York Times* columnist, and simply surrender, knowing I will never reach his level. At the risk of hyperbole, I can say I would consider my life less complete had I never read these opening lines from his *All Over but the Shoutin'* (my favorite nonfiction work):

My mother and father were born in the most beautiful place on earth, in the foothills of the Appalachians along the Alabama-Georgia line. It was a place where gray mists hid the tops of low, deep-green mountains, where redbone and bluetick hounds dashed through the pines as they chased possums into the sacks of old men in frayed overalls, where old women in bonnets dipped Bruton snuff and hummed "Faded Love and Winter Roses" as they shelled purple hulls, canned peaches and made biscuits too good for this world. It was a place where playing the church piano loud was near as important as playing it right, where fearless young men steered long, black Buicks loaded with yellow whiskey down roads the color of dried blood, where the first frost meant hog killin' time and the mouthwatering smell of cracklin's would drift for acres from giant, bubbling pots.

That's one book that makes me *want* to read a paragraph twice, just because of its power and poetry. I recommend it to any writer at any stage of the journey.

I also believe the words of Christ to Martha in John 11:25–26 are among the most beautiful ever translated into English: "I am the resurrection and the life. He that believes in me, though he were dead, yet shall he live. And he that lives and believes in me shall never die." Even if I didn't believe those words, I'd find them wonderfully rendered.

Truth be told, I am a writer who uses description sparingly, because I find it deadly boring unless it's like Charles Frazier crafts it in his debut masterpiece, *Cold Mountain*. But description is not his only genius. The novel follows Inman, a Confederate deserter, as he journeys hundreds of miles on foot to return to his sweetheart. The scene below takes place en route, when a kind stranger named Sarah, an eighteen-year-old widow, cooks him a meal. Here's a taste of Frazier's prose:

> [Her] baby had a croupy cough. Inman figured there was little
> reason to expect it to come out the other side of winter alive.
> It fretted in Sarah's arms and would not sleep, and so she
> sang it a song. She sang as if shamed by her own sounds, by
> the way her life voiced itself aloud. As she began, it seemed
> a blockage had set up in her throat, and so the chant that
> escaped her did so with much effort. The force of air from her
> chest needed somewhere to go, but finding the jaw set firm
> and jutted and the mouth clenched against music, it took
> the far way out and reached expression in high nasal tones
> that hurt to hear in their loneliness. The singing carried shrill
> into the twilight and its tones spoke of despair, resentment,
> an undertone of panic. Her singing against such resistance
> seemed to Inman about the greatest thing he had ever wit-
> nessed. It was like watching a bitter fight carried to a costly
> draw. The sound of her was that of a woman of the previous
> century living out in the present, that old and weary. Sarah
> was such a child to sound that way.

Stephen King, another of my favorite authors, has a great ear for dialogue. More than that, he works description into the action, nuanced as part of the story. You don't realize until later that you saw, smelled, and felt the scene. He forces the reader to use all five senses and knows what to leave out.

I have said that some of the best writing around is sports writing and that the best examples of that are in *Sports Illustrated*. Here's proof from William Nack, a former horse-racing writer for the magazine, from his piece on the great Secretariat. For days after discovering this pristine paragraph, which wonderfully makes use of horse-racing vernacular, I obliged friends and family to listen as I read. I covered quarter-horse racing as a sportswriter, but have never attended a thoroughbred race in person. And yet this exquisite piece of writing still moves me:

Oh, I knew all the stories. Knew them well. Had crushed and rolled them in my hand until their quaint musk lay in the saddle of my palm. Knew them as I knew the stories of my children. Knew them as I knew the stories of my own life. Told them at dinner parties. Swapped them with horseplayers as if they were trading cards. Argued over them with old men and blind fools who had seen the show, but missed the message. Dreamed them and turned them over like pillows in my rubbery sleep. Woke up with them. Brushed my aging teeth with them. Grinned at them in the mirror. Horses had a way of getting inside you, and so it was that Secretariat became like a fifth child in our house. The older boy who was off at school and never around, but who was as loved and true a part of the family as Muffin, our shaggy epileptic dog.

Clearly that was not something William Nack dashed off. Hours of thought and polish made it shine.

Several years ago, *The Civil War* aired on PBS. The Ken Burns special included a letter written by Major Sullivan Ballou, a volunteer in the Second Rhode Island Regiment, to his wife a week before the bloody Battle of Bull Run in Manassas. Thirty-two years old, Ballou was a lawyer. He wrote the letter from Camp Clark, just outside the nation's capital, on July 14, 1861. Excerpts from the letter appear below.

> My very dear Sarah:
> The indications are very strong that we shall move in a few days—perhaps tomorrow. Lest I should not be able to write again, I feel impelled to write a few lines that may fall under your eye when I shall be no more ...

Sarah my love for you is deathless, it seems to bind me with mighty cables that nothing but Omnipotence could break; and yet my love of Country comes over me like a strong wind and bears me unresistibly on with all these chains to the battle field.

The memories of the blissful moments I have spent with you come creeping over me, and I feel most gratified to God and to you that I have enjoyed them for so long. And hard it is for me to give them up and burn to ashes the hopes of future years, when, God willing, we might still have lived and loved together, and seen our sons grown up to honorable manhood, around us. I have, I know, but few and small claims upon Divine Providence, but something whispers to me—perhaps it is the wafted prayer of my little Edgar, that I shall return to my loved ones unharmed. If I do not my dear Sarah, never forget how much I love you, and when my last breath escapes me on the battle field, it will whisper your name. Forgive my many faults and the many pains I have caused you. How thoughtless and foolish I have often times been! How gladly would I wash out with my tears every little spot upon your happiness ...

But, O Sarah! If the dead can come back to this earth and flit unseen around those they loved, I shall always be near you; in the gladdest days and in the darkest nights ... always, always, and if there be a soft breeze upon your cheek, it shall be my breath, as the cool air fans your throbbing temple, it shall be my spirit passing by. Sarah do not mourn me dead; think I am gone and wait for thee, for we shall meet again....

Major Sullivan Ballou was killed in the Battle of Bull Run.

Imagine that from a man who did not even make his living as a writer. Apparently society did something unique back then. They must have taught reading and writing in school.

HARRY POTTER'S MAGIC

J.K. Rowling's Harry Potter books are well written, vivid, and creative. Rowling is another author who makes the reader uses all five senses. The story of a boy with magical powers reflects every child's dream. Will he be able to control those powers and fight against evil? The story grabs you from the start and never lets go.

Many worry about what such stories might teach children, but I put the Potter books in the same category as *The Wizard of Oz*. I was raised on the latter, and I was never tempted toward witchcraft. I knew it was pure fantasy, and I enjoyed being entertained.

Most kids will no more think Harry Potter is real than they will believe Mary Poppins was. Of course, if you're worried about your children reading it, wait until you believe they're old enough; you might begin by reading it to them and discussing it. If your child is still young enough to be confused or misled, it's your responsibility to monitor what she reads. You'll know when your child can differentiate between fantasy and reality.

To my mind, much of the opposition to the Potter books is an embarrassment. It's okay to caution parents about the content for young kids, but there's no call for personally attacking the author. And have the decency to read a book before bashing it.

Q & A WITH JERRY

Do you enjoy learning new words?

I do, but it's important to generally lean toward the familiar word in your writing. Readers like to learn, as long as they don't have to constantly consult the dictionary. Use a fresh word in a familiar format—where its meaning is obvious—and your readers will thank you.

Because I love anagrams, I'm good at the Jumble, that puzzle in the newspaper that requires you to unscramble four words. That's a good exercise for a wordsmith, which we writers should be. When I'm hot, I can do all four words within ten seconds. Naturally, one of them occasionally hangs me up for several minutes. One recent anagram had me baffled for a long time until the solution finally came to me: *author*. Drove me nuts.

I use a lot of anagrams in my books. Paul Stepola's last name is an anagram, as are others in the Soon series. I do that for my own amusement, but it's fun when readers notice. Sometimes I'll give hints, but I never come out and tell them.

What's the origin of your Scrabble obsession?

My mother and her family always liked Scrabble. Especially my grandfather. I didn't like the game at first, because it seemed slow to me. The family played recreationally with up to four players, no time limits, and dictionary checking allowed during play. The games took forever.

Dianna and I had young kids when I discovered the strange world of Scrabble clubs. One met near my office, and I was almost immediately hooked by the precise rules. It was head-to-head (just two people), with a chess clock (each player gets twenty-five minutes per game), no referring to dictionaries except on challenges—and the loser of a challenge lost his next turn. I began playing once a week, and soon began playing in tournaments all over the country, winning championships in five states. I must clarify, however, that I was never a top player. As in chess, there are several levels, and I was winning at my level, which was in the middle somewhere. The top players study word lists constantly and could toy with me.

To really compete in clubs and tournaments, a player must know all the legal two- and three-letter words—like *aa*, a type of lava. *Ai* is a Greek letter. *Ae* means "one." Most people wouldn't know those three, let alone several others that appear strange. The higher your level, the more of the four-, five-, six-, seven-, and even eight-letter words you must know.

Few neighborhood or recreational players want to challenge me now, and I don't have time for club competition, so I usually play on the computer.

Are you also a crossword puzzle fan?

Only a fair-weather fan, when I'm in the mood. My dad worked a crossword puzzle every day. My problem is that once I start I'm obsessed with getting every word without help.

Boggle is my favorite word game, because it's fast and I can play it on the computer. I play my sons, each of us at a different computer. Many writers naturally like word games like that.

Is there an objective standard for good writing?

Probably not, but like most people—I think—I appreciate clean, concise, uncluttered prose that's easy to read and understand. The most common comment I get is that my writing reads too easily. But that's intentional. It's hard work to write clearly. I've long said I wish I were smart enough to write a book that's hard to read.

How can a young writer succeed?

In any writer, I look for the *-ilities*: humility, teachability, coachability, availability, and flexibility.

What will make or break you is developing a thick skin. Can you work with an editor, or are you offended by every suggestion? When you've queried an editor and gotten a tentative green light (in other words, when she has told you she will consider your submission on speculation), that's your opportunity to show off your -*ilities*.

In the New Testament, Paul writes to Timothy that he should not let anyone despise him because of his youth. He meant this in a spiritual sense, and was urging his protégé to not let his young age get in the way of his missionary work. But this is good counsel for writers too. No one is ever too young to come up with a captivating story. The Christian Writers Guild has created two courses for young writers—Pages (for ages eight through twelve) and Squires (for ages thirteen and up). These courses offer intense training in writing essentials. (If you fit these age groups or know a budding writer who does, check us out at www.ChristianWritersGuild.com.)

I was writing at an early age, though I made typical mistakes, like starting an article with the date: "On Saturday, August 18th, the Fighting Falcons ... " I cringe when I see my teenage output.

My mother knew a real newspaper sports writer and showed him my clippings. All I wanted was praise and "Where has he been all our lives?" But the *Chicago Tribune* writer thought I was looking for an honest critique. "Start with the meat," he said.

"Not with the date." And he went on from there, giving invaluable input. It hurt, but truth hurts. And instructs.

I used to cover high school wrestling meets. From my perspective, the same things happened in every match. Guys rolled around, sweated, and tried to pin each other. For some reason, I thought it was creative to say, "Johnson edged Thompson," or "Bailey slaughtered Smith." I would have someone "massacre" one opponent or "squeak by" another. Every single verb was painfully colorful. I should have simply listed who won and how and left it at that.

Sometimes creative writing teachers show me their favorite students' work, and these often prove to be ridiculously flowery samples with endless description. When I suggest teaching the students to back away from the overuse of adjectives, the instructors stiffen. "That shows creativity," they say. "I want them to be expressive." I think to myself, *I guess you also want them not to sell.*

There's a place, of course, for limitless creativity with little thought to structure. But then students should be pointed to examples of simple, straightforward prose that works—and sells.

Can someone be too old to start writing?

The odds can be against you if you wait too long, because your style may come across as dated, especially if you write as you did in school decades ago. But there are notable exceptions. Dr. Sherwood Wirt, longtime editor for *Decision* magazine, wrote well into his nineties, but you sure couldn't tell that from his stuff. He produced crisp copy, the sure sign of a craftsman.

I discovered a writer in her late sixties who had not been published. Nancy Bayless went from writing a few articles for me when I was editor of *Moody* magazine to becoming widely published and a mentor to other writers.

As judge of the inspirational category of *Writer's Digest's* annual writing competition, I have twice awarded first place to a man in his seventies who will soon have his first novel published.

Any thoughts on the romance genre?

I'm on thin ice when I talk about romance novels, especially in the inspirational field. And I have many beloved colleagues who are more than successful in this field. The ones I appreciate somehow avoid the dreadfully formulaic.

There's nothing wrong with including elements of romance in your writing. Love is a rich part of life. I fear that society's fascination with potboiler romances, though, says more about the readers than it does about the writing. Many romance readers are fanatics, flying through several books a week. They know all the authors and obsess over the details of the period settings, not to mention the conventions of the genre—when the main characters must meet (within so many pages), that they must both be gorgeous, that they must be initially repulsed by each other, etc.

The genre has come a long way from many of those stereotypes, and I'm for anything that encourages reading.

BRETT BUTLER

Working with Brett Butler, the former Los Angeles Dodgers outfielder, who for years was the player in the big leagues with the smallest shoe size (seven), brought me back to my favorite sport in 1997. Brett, who would finish his career with the most infield hits of any player in the history of the game, had a story that transcended baseball. He was a cancer survivor.

He developed throat cancer at the beginning of one season, had surgery and treatment, was rehabilitated, worked himself back into shape, then actually rejoined the Dodgers the same season. No one, including his loved ones, could believe it. Then, ironically, he was injured and had to miss the end of the season. Brett decided it was God's way of telling him, "You accomplished something, but you really need to take more time off."

Brett and I were working on his book together when the next season opened, and he escorted me on a tour through the bowels of Dodger Stadium at Chavez Ravine in Los Angeles. There we happened upon pitching star Curt Schilling, then the ace of the Philadelphia Phillies. He would be the opposing starter for that opening game. He and Brett were friends, and it was fun to see them interact.

Schilling, who was six-four and well over two hundred pounds, towered over the diminutive Butler. He said something to Brett about that day being Brett's big comeback.

"Yeah," Brett said, "take it easy on me, huh?"

Schilling, known for being a fierce competitor (not unlike Butler), smiled and said, "I'll put one in your ear."

As we moved on, I said, "He's funny."

Brett gave me a look. "He was dead serious," he said.

Butler led off for the Dodgers in the bottom of the first inning, and the first pitch was high and tight. Friendship ends in the tunnels.

CHAPTER
8

Realism Through Research

Okay, you're equipped and holed up and ready to roll. Don't even think about starting your writing before doing your research.

Your story may be fictitious, but your details had better be correct. I mean, what would you think if you were reading an otherwise engrossing novel and came across this line: "When President John F. Kennedy was assassinated in Dallas, Texas had been a state for just fifteen years"?

Excuse me? Everyone knows Kennedy was shot in November of 1963. So Texas came into the Union in 1948? All right, that's a rather egregious error. It took me sixty seconds to find the state's Web site and learn that Texas was annexed to the United States as the twenty-eighth state in 1845, seceded and joined the Confederacy in 1861, and was readmitted to the Union in 1870.

When I make mistakes, I hear from readers. Get lazy, and experts will come out of the woodwork. These people scrutinize not only factual details—especially in their areas of expertise—they also challenge flaws in logic. And as a writer, when you're wrong, you're wrong. Better to just admit it and fix it for the next printing than try to explain it away. I once got several comments from ex-military personnel telling me that I had given a main character a rank he couldn't have earned with the background I had outlined for him. It had slipped past my editors and even my technical consultant, but I take full responsibility. My name's on the cover. And people are watching.

Reader buy-in can be affected, positively or negatively, by well-researched details. I can make up a futuristic device that does something that cannot be done today, but it had better be plausible. My technical consultants tell me that if you can imagine something, it will likely be on the market in five years, but there are logical limits. What if I had a character fashion a gun out of ice that could shoot a projectile a half mile? That would so stretch the bounds of credibility that I would lose readers.

The story, once your premise has been accepted, must be logical. The technical details have to fit. And anachronisms will jar every time. (*Anachronism* is one of my favorite words. *Chronos* is the root word and means "time." *Ana* means "out of.") One of my hobbies is to look for anachronisms—details out of place and time—in movies, stage plays, and novels. For instance, an American flag bearing fifty stars hanging on the wall of an office in the 1930s. Or, in a movie set in the 1950s, a suburban street with ramps carved out of the curbs at intersections so wheelchairs can maneuver easily.

Any American flag made from 1912 to 1959 would bear only forty-eight stars; Alaska and Hawaii were added in 1959. And laws requiring consideration of the disabled are fairly recent developments, too.

In a movie I saw that was set in the late 1930s, a housewife pulled a Tupperware container from the refrigerator. It made me wonder. A quick check on the Internet told me Tupperware made its debut in 1946. Careful writers avoid such gaffes.

TIME TRAVEL

I may be known for futuristic fiction, in which virtually anything goes—within reason. But one of my toughest writing chores was re-creating the infancy of the twentieth century for *Though None Go With Me*.

I'm familiar with the geographic setting; I grew up near Three Rivers, Michigan. My mother attended high school there; my parents were married there. But in a novel set in 1900, the period is as important as the place and nearly as important as the characters.

I had to live in the archives of the Three Rivers library for days, and even then could make only educated guesses at how long it would have taken to travel between Three Rivers and Kalamazoo, for instance, before Oakland Drive and U.S. Route 131 existed.

Also, in a saga that covers sixty-five years, World War I comes into play. The flu epidemic of 1918 and 1919. Eventually, World War II. I found fascinating details, like the designations people put in their windows if their offspring were at war.

The more recent the period of the story, the more readers who would remember the period. I discovered that the Three Rivers fire department had once divided the town into four sections, and my research told me that the First Ward was considered *the* place to live. My mother remembered this and was surprised that I reflected the cultural differences between the Three Rivers wards.

Living witnesses were an enormous help. I discovered that the community had indeed lost many citizens to the flu epidemic. Schools shut down, even doctors died. To write about a woman born in 1900 and growing up in Three Rivers, without mentioning the flu epidemic when she was eighteen, would have been a huge gaffe. I made the tragedy a major part of the story, as it remains a stark memory for my sources, who were children then.

My research freed and assured me. When I set a pivotal accident on a certain roadway, my research confirmed the route was in existence at that time in the story. *But,* you say, *it's fiction. Couldn't you have made up a road?* Sure, but why not place the events where they *could* have happened? Readers, especially those from that area, easily suspended disbelief because they imagined the events as if they were true.

I wrote about the Bonnie Castle, mentioned in history books but no longer standing. Believe me, I looked for it. I tapped the recollections of older residents, who told me Bonnie Castle was originally a residence, then a hospital, then a library before it was finally torn down. I made sure I had it in the right spot and being used for the right purpose for the period. Many would have called me on it if I had tried to bluff.

My mother recalled that the older kids in school always picked on the younger kids, calling them names. The epithet of choice when she was in high school in the 1940s? The upper classmen called the freshman *Rhinies.* It didn't take much research to confirm that this was short for *Rhinelander,* the general name for the inhabitants of the land on both sides of the river Rhine in the west of Germany. American kids certainly didn't want to be called Germans during World War II. Working that tidbit into the story made it come alive for readers my mother's age.

Where fiction left fact was in the establishment of Elisabeth's church. I did make up the church—primarily because, if I didn't make it a particular denomination, I could be open about its strengths and weaknesses without stepping on toes. I called it Christ Church, but various readers were certain it was their church. Some said they were sure it was the Methodist Church, saying, "I know, because I went there." Others believed it was yet another church. I purposely located the church where there has never been a building.

Research will also reveal specific businesses and landmarks that can make your story more realistic. I have my main character working at Snyder's Drugs to try to make ends meet. Readers remembered the place fondly but didn't remember the character. I wonder why.

I based much of the dialogue and speech patterns on dialogue in old movies. I thought we spoke quickly today because of our fast-paced lives, but the black-and-whites from the 1930s and 1940s reveal people talking every bit as fast.

I was criticized by several readers (particularly elderly women) for making my main character fairly decrepit by age sixty-five. Elisabeth had arthritis, and her eyesight was almost gone. *She's too young to seem so old*, readers wrote. Of course, they were responding out of their own experience. Today, sixty-five is considered late middle age, and we expect to remain active into our eighties.

But here's where my research rescued me. At the time in which I set the story, people in their late sixties were considered ancient. A woman born in 1900 had a life expectancy of seventy-one. I'm delighted that people are living longer, healthier lives (I'm within a decade of sixty-five myself), but I had to be faithful to reality in my novel.

My signing in Three Rivers (a town of seven thousand residents) was one of my best ever. Hundreds lined up on the main street, and the event had to be moved from the tiny bookstore to a hall next door. I met people who knew my grandparents, my mother, my aunt (who still lived there), and many who had worked at the factory prominent in the story. One woman even brought me a framed photograph of Bonnie Castle.

I've said that any published piece of writing is not a solo, but a duet between editor and author. My editor saved me from a huge embarrassment in *Though None Go With Me*. A major plot element concerns one of Elisabeth's sons coming home from World War II traumatized to the point of muteness by the horrors he witnessed while fighting in the Pacific Theater. When he finally finds his voice, he rasps, "I killed Germans."

"No wonder he was struck dumb," my editor noted in the margins. "He would have killed only Japanese in the Pacific Theater."

Right, I knew that. I was just testing him.

For those mistakes your editor is not likely to catch, you may want to find outside help. You may not be at a place where you can pay a consultant, but you rarely have to. Find an expert in a certain field, ask if he'll look at your manuscript to be sure you're on track technically, and promise only the mention of his name in the acknowledgments. I'd be surprised if you didn't get as much diligence as if you were paying by the hour.

And most such experts are founts of ideas that can make your story even better. I'm constantly asking my aviation consultant what would happen in this or that scenario, and he often comes up with real-life examples. What could be better than that?

ALMANACS AND ATLASES

Almanacs and atlases are wonderful, inexpensive investments. A world almanac is a must for the serious writer, and if you can afford one on disk, so much the better; you'll be relieved of the tiny print in the paperback versions, and of course you'll decrease your look-up time.

World almanacs include just about anything you could ever want in the way of basic research. I even use them for coming up with character names. When naming a foreign character, I'll look up his country of origin, scan the current government leaders for a last name, combine that with a first name from the country's history (say, a war hero), and bingo, I have a perfectly legitimate and ethnically accurate name.

I use a world atlas primarily because my characters travel the globe, and to be believable, I have to know the time zones, the current country names (which seem to change often), the monetary unit, population, average temperatures, and the like.

Atlases provide detailed maps, and Internet atlases offer even street maps—crucial to action scenes. But almanacs also give the gross national product, offer tourism tidbits, and list major industries and resources. In the Left Behind series, I set some scenes in Greece, a country I've never visited. The almanac told me that one of Greece's natural resources is lignite. A couple more keystrokes in Google, and I discovered that lignite is a type of coal used to generate electrical power. I needed an occupation for a wealthy Greek. So he became a lignite magnate.

I didn't get one letter from a Greek reader asking what the heck the lignite thing was all about.

Almanacs also show which countries are on the metric system, so when my character is racing through a metrics-using country in a rental car, he is going to buy fuel in liters and calculate fuel usage in liters per 100 kilometers rather than in miles per gallon. Getting minuscule details like that right makes for a more entertaining read. And when you get them wrong, suddenly they're no longer minuscule.

If necessary, you can find free almanacs, dictionaries, and encyclopedias online. Simply Google *almanac* or *dictionary* and see what your options are. Some sites require a subscription, but before you pay, make sure you'll actually use the product. Check for a trial period or a free alternative.

I use an electronic thesaurus, which is a good aid but also merits a caution: Never let it be obvious you've consulted a thesaurus. Novice writers tend to seek the most exotic word, when the best use of a thesaurus is to remind yourself of alternative ordinary words. Look for the one that best conveys your intention.

Believe me, readers can tell when you've fallen into a rut and overused a favorite word. They'll let you know.

DIGGING EVEN DEEPER

Research takes you only so far. Eventually you have to push past cold facts and go beyond your research to create your own world and its inhabitants.

Even though my character Elisabeth was a young woman early in the twentieth century, I had to look within myself for some of her motivations and flaws. I could sure identify with someone who wasn't perfect but who wanted to be obedient. Often she failed and reacted in ways she shouldn't have, because I do the same.

Because I was "raised in the church," as those of my ilk are wont to say, I recall wondering at a very young age what it really meant to be a godly person. I was one of those kids who loved everything about church and Sunday school. Some writers remember hating that part of life, and their recollections make for interesting, often dark, fiction.

But I have learned that even those who didn't rebel against or suffer from the downside of a religious upbringing can also face the conflicts crucial to good fiction. The story of a little goody-two-shoes who grows up to be a pastor or a missionary would not likely make an interesting novel until the character faces opposition in the church or on the mission field. We can complain all we want about how good stories don't get enough attention, but the fact is, conflict makes fiction more interesting.

So my what-if for my main character, Elisabeth, became *What if she was truly devout and suffered for it, like Job?* That's where it got fun, because I have to say I have barely suffered for my faith. But I have traveled to countries where religion has been suppressed, and I've seen people—even in my own country—who, despite their devotion, seem to suffer more than most. Drawing from that, I was able to throw chaos into Elisabeth's life that would have caused a lesser person—not a heroine—to turn her back on her faith. And, of course, Elisabeth almost does. When everything dear to her has been ripped away, she is left with the choice of the ages: remain faithful to a God who seems to have abandoned her, or abandon herself to Him.

I see my work in two parts, divided by a huge box car on the railroad tracks of my mind. I spend days filling the box car with raw materials from one side of the tracks, then I make my way around to the other side and begin unloading the box car into my manuscript. There is scrap here and there, lots of waste, but also nuggets that prove to be pure gold. And when I mix and match stuff that went in wholly unconnected, I usually find more than enough for a good story.

A serious caution here: Make sure your research comes through to the reader subtly, as texture for your story, not as evidence that you did your homework. The research gets in the way of the story in the example below:

> "You know, Fred," Christine said, "thirty-seven percent of these types of criminals are recidivists, and even those who complete a halfway-house program find themselves back in prison thirteen percent of the time."

"That's true, Christine. I've heard that three states have insti-
tuted measures to try to rehabilitate these guys. Regardless of
the therapy they receive, they have to have a two-thirds major-
ity vote of the parole board in order to ..."

Now see how the research merely flavors this scene:

"You hear Michaels is out of prison?" Fred said.
    Christine shook her head. "Two-to-one he's back in the
joint within six months. He ought to be glad he didn't get
busted in Indiana. No parole there for this anymore."

The more you dump into your boxcar storehouse, the more you'll
have to work with when you're on the other side of the tracks.
So do your research, fill your idea storehouse, then get to work.

MIKE SINGLETARY AND JOE GIBBS

I enjoyed an unusual opportunity one year when a publisher asked me to write two football books, one on Mike Singletary of the Chicago Bears and one on Joe Gibbs, coach of the Washington Redskins. When I saw that the teams were scheduled to play one another, I suggested the publisher send me to that game to kill two birds with one stone. Fortunately for me, the game was in Washington, so I got a nice trip out of it as well.

Singletary and Gibbs each offered sideline passes. I would get to experience the game from ground level, in the midst of players, coaches, and officials. That was a wonderful prospect for one who would rather watch on TV than from bad seats far from the field at live games.

The question then became which offer to accept. Should I risk Gibbs seeing me on the Bears sideline, or Singletary seeing me on the Redskins sideline? Put aside for the moment that I had forgotten the competitive nature of these people; they would have a lot more on their minds than where I stood, and neither would likely notice.

I spent the pre-game with Coach Gibbs in his office, the game on the Bears sidelines, and the post-game in the Redskins locker room. Each venue brought unforgettable images and helped make the books, *Singletary on Singletary* and *Joe Gibbs: Fourth and One*, that much more realistic.

For the next several days, many friends asked if it had been me they'd seen on TV, standing near the Bears place kicker as he warmed up. "A big guy with a beard and a hat. Was it you?"

"Yes," I'd say. "Just doing a little coaching."

Being that close to the action gave me a perspective I hadn't had since covering high school sports. Every time players crashed into each other, they hit so hard they involuntarily grunted like wild animals.

Regardless of your subject, during the research phase, get as close to the action as possible. It'll show in your writing.

Joe Gibbs, who took an eleven-year hiatus from coaching the Redskins to run his own NASCAR racing team, insisted that one thing be included in his life story: He said that, wherever he went to speak, he always finished by telling people how he had become a Christian and how they could too. He wanted to add that message to the end of the story as an epilogue, and to urge readers to come to faith in Christ.

Everyone, me included, tried to talk him out of this. I reasoned that he had already told his own conversion story, and that it came naturally in the story and made its point. If a reader was moved to convert, he certainly would. The publisher and editor agreed.

But Joe would not be dissuaded. "It's the whole point," he said, "and I want it crystal clear and to tell the reader how to do it."

The publisher announced what they thought was their final decision: no. The book worked as it was; the epilogue was inappropriate and overkill.

So Joe announced his final decision. Despite having been most cooperative and easy to work with, he said he felt so strongly about this point that he would return the advance and pull the plug if the book didn't end the way he wished. The publisher blinked. And the supplementary material proved most effective and was the subject of most of our fan mail.

As for Mike Singletary, I'll never forget interviewing him in the den in his home. Few people realized—myself included—that he was hard of hearing and used hearing aids in both ears. I always urge subjects to sit where they're comfortable, and then I choose a spot facing them. I got Mike wired up and told him to sit anywhere, so he chose right next to me.

Having one of the fiercest linebackers in the history of the National Football League nearly rubbing knees with you can affect what questions you ask and how you ask them.

He is such a serious and spiritual man that it didn't surprise me when he said he tried "to pour spiritual truth into [his] children every day." What did surprise me was finding out that the eldest of his children was just seven years old at the time. I could just imagine him telling them stories, reading to them, praying with them, teaching them.

Mike also turned out to be one of the most self-revelatory subjects I have ever interviewed, revealing tremendous shortcomings of character in his past and insisting on dealing with them in the book. In fact, he told of having been unfaithful to his wife when they were engaged, and how he had felt compelled to confess during their honeymoon. His account of watching his wife disintegrate emotionally before his eyes was heartrending for me to hear—and for him to tell. He realized that he would have to prove himself to her anew, gain her forgiveness and trust, and start to rebuild their relationship on truth.

When the manuscript was in Mike's hands for final tweaking, advisers must have gotten to him and told him he had been too frank. The text came back to me wholly watered down and tentative sounding, with the power and frankness of the real Mike Singletary missing. That was the first and only time I conspired with the publisher—in this case, my old friend Bruce Barbour, my editor at Thomas Nelson—to somehow wrangle the story back to its original intensity.

Bruce simply got on the phone and asked Mike, "What happened to the distinctive personality I was hearing from in the first version? All the life has been sucked out of this."

Mike, always deliberate, thoughtful, and decisive, was silent for several seconds. Finally he said, "You're the expert. Go with the original."

CHAPTER 9

Pace, Conflict, and Plot

The pacing of a good piece of writing is akin to a ride on a roller coaster. The highlights may be the big whoosh on the way down or the dizzying loops of the new monsters of the midway. But you'd be shortsighted to forget that half the fun is in the anticipation, that slow clacking up to the apex, where spines tingle, breathing stalls, and hearts pound.

In an article or a book, you need to incorporate changes of pace. Slower periods allow the reader to get her bearings, and the writer to convey important information that might be lost during a breathless action scene. But, like the architect of a good roller coaster ride, be sure to provide enough tension and buildup so your rider (reader) doesn't lose interest. That halting trip to the top may be the slowest part of the ride, but no one is getting off because they're bored, are they?

CONFLICT

When I get the niggling feeling that my story has been too quiet for too long, I'll force competing characters together. Or I'll kill somebody.

Or I'll realize that I have used several pages just to get a character from one place to another, and mercilessly hack that to half a page. Believe me, tightening is almost *always* an improvement. Imagine your reader constantly urging you to get on with the story.

Conflict helps create what novel-writing guru Sol Stein calls the engine of a story. It's what makes the story move, what makes the reader wonder what happens next. Any time I find myself floundering and I feel the story has stalled, I put two characters in the same room, get them talking, and have one say something wholly out of character.

Maybe they're idyllic lovers and have barely ever had a spat. Or they're best friends who always give each other the benefit of the doubt. But in this scene, one of them erupts: "You always say that! And you're wrong, as usual."

Put yourself in the other's shoes. You're shocked. What brought this on? Maybe you think of an annoyance you could throw out to add fuel to the fire. Inject conflict, and the story is off and running again.

Any obstacle has the potential to cause conflict. If you get up in the morning for a job interview and your phone and car are dead, what are you going to do? That's conflict.

Resist the urge to fix everything so your protagonist has clear sailing. It's tempting to give a private eye a rich client or some other source of unlimited funds, so she can pursue a case without worrying about paying the rent. Better to go the other way. Have her evicted, living with friends, unable to get her clothes cleaned, wondering where her next meal will come from. That's conflict, and it will move your story forward.

Conflict is crucial. Conflict is indispensable.

Conflict also creates tension. Two characters strive for the same goal, be it the same woman or the same job. One of them may be more sympathetic, but don't make that too obvious. You might not even know yourself who wins until the story plays out.

Put best friends up for the same prize in a prestigious piano competition: Joe likes Stacy and cares about her, but he also believes he is more talented.

Stacy has already received high marks. Joe enters late—not his fault (conflict, tension)—and is stressed, sweating. He doesn't do well under such conditions. The judges are clearly irritated at the delay. Stacy sits smugly, eager. The two pretend not to care who wins, but the reader knows better.

Now what if Joe stumbles and loses, then discovers something that leads him to believe that Stacy sabotaged him? Better for your story: It's not true. Now you have an intriguing tale.

Have fun with the what-if game. It's a novelist's lifeblood.

WHERE DO YOU GET YOUR PLOT IDEAS?

People ask me all the time where I get my ideas. Readers want to know if I get my ideas at the keyboard. Do I see the action and describe it? Yes, for me, that's how it happens. I have found that about half the novelists I know are outliners and half are not. I fall into the second category. Knowing the sales of friends and colleagues and acquaintances, I can say with confidence that neither formula is better than the other. Some need the safety net of an outline. Some outline so completely that manuscript preparation becomes the filling in of blanks, and yet somehow it works.

I write as a process of discovery. I write to find out what happens next, figuring that if the story surprises and delights or shocks and scares me, it should have the same effect on the reader. The last thing a novelist wants to be is predictable, and it can be a good thing if even she doesn't know for sure where the story is going.

Writing as a process of discovery gives me an out when readers demand to know why I killed off their favorite character. I say, "I didn't kill him off; I found him dead."

I put the characters on the page, give them opposing goals or opinions, and let the consequences play out in my mind as I record what happens. Some thought it heresy when Stephen King reported in his book *On Writing* that, in essence, plot is overrated. He's of the school that dreams up interesting people and situations and then follows the action. After reading dozens of experts' ideas on how to manufacture plots, I celebrated when I read King. How much better to follow the story than to contrive it.

Sometimes I make a note or two to remind myself to finish a thought or a puzzle, but that's as close as I come to outlining. I am often amazed when something I inserted with no conscious reason—something I was both willing and prepared to delete at a later stage, if necessary—turns out to have had some reason after all. That's the subconscious doing its work.

I began *Left Behind* with the line, "Rayford Steele's mind was on a woman he had never touched." I then immediately had to establish that he was piloting a 747, had a wife and kids, and yet was daydreaming about a possible affair. That's on the edges of risqué for a novel in the inspirational market, but it was chaste enough to work. And the very elements that made the publishing house wonder if it was too close to the edge seemed to help the novel succeed.

Other books of mine start with different tones. I needed a long view (the way many movies begin) to establish the setting and tone for my Christmas romance—about Santa, of all things (a risky theme for a Christian writer)—which I intended as a parable of faith.

The first paragraph from *'Twas the Night Before*:

> Snow sweet-talked its way into Chicago in broad daylight the
> day after Thanksgiving. Huge, splatty flakes conspired to blan-
> ket, then cripple the city. By dark Chicago moved in slushy
> slow motion.

A couple of paragraphs later, the reader meets one of the two main
characters in a restaurant:

> Tom over-tipped, gathered up the competing *Sun-Times* and
> his notebook, and stepped into the mess. By the time he set-
> tled in to write his column, "Douten, Thomas," the snow in
> his hair had melted and was running down his neck.

I wanted to make the reader cold as she read, and I strove for the visual and tactile. In one sentence, she learns that Tom is generous, wor-
ries about the competition, and is a writer. Giving the reader credit, I
gradually reveal more—that he's a glass-half-empty guy who meets a
glass-half-full woman who still literally believes in Santa Claus.

If I had started with: "Tom Douten was a cynical newspaper columnist who always wrote about down-and-outers but fell in love with a
Pollyanna girl who still believed in Santa Claus," I would have been
spoon-feeding the reader what she would rather discover on her own.

Hemingway was the master at allowing his reader to discover the
story, of course. He might start a scene with something like, "The
woman always ...," knowing full well we have no idea who this person is. But we want to know, especially if she is "always" doing something in particular. Is the perspective character her husband? The setting and the conflict gradually take shape, and we learn what we need
as we go. From the dialogue, we discover the woman is grieving a
death, and we get the fun of discovering additional details along the

way. Hemingway made readers feel as if they were an integral part of the whole deal. You have to read carefully and notice, and the story will eventually make sense.

Give readers enough to stay curious, but let them figure things out for themselves. Don't tell or even show everything. The woman cuts bread, a boy delivers the *Paris Review*. The streets are cobblestone. The writer doesn't have to come out and say where the story is set. Avoid clunky exposition; strive for subtlety.

THAT WILLING SUSPENSION OF DISBELIEF

The more you study writing, the more you'll run across the phrase *suspension of disbelief*. It has been traced to Samuel Taylor Coleridge. He asked of his readers "that willing suspension of disbelief for the moment that constitutes poetic faith." In other words, readers are to temporarily choose not to disbelieve what might otherwise trip up their logical minds. Some have called this *emphatic belief*.

In my novella *'Twas the Night Before*, my main character—a cynic to the point of doubt and disdain—barely survives a plane crash in Germany's Black Forest. He is rescued by elves, who ferry him to Santa's complex. By portraying Tom Douten as thoroughly convinced he has gone mad, I am asking the reader to come in on the secret with me: The fact is that he is not crazy, not dead, and that this is no dream, no hallucination. Rather, his former fiancée has been right all along: Santa is real.

Should you ever run across this little tome—one of my favorite labors of love, by the way—judge for yourself whether I stretched too far the bounds of credulity. But you see what I'm driving at. No adult reads this and sincerely changes her mind about the literal existence of Santa. All I'm asking is what any novelist asks: a temporary, willing suspension of disbelief. Without it, the spell is lost.

While I'm on this subject, let me add that one of my disappointments with too much contemporary fiction—especially, I'm afraid, in the inspirational market—is a propensity for novelists to intrude on the fictitious construct itself. Too many begin their novels with dedications and acknowledgments so long that they delay too much the dive into their imaginative world. And often they compound this with a page or two of where they got the idea, what they hope the reader learns from the story, and why it was so much fun to write—because of all the interesting people they met during the research.

I urge you to get out of the way of your reader and her visit to your created world. That's what she paid for. That's what she carved time for. That's why she's settled before the fire with a cup. A line of dedication to someone special, a word of thanks to another for her help, and then, please, chapter one, paragraph one, line one.

There's also the danger of over-explaining the story from the beginning. As I said before, let it play out. Don't tell exactly who everyone is or what the mystery or problem is. Readers love to discover the story as they go. Of course, you don't want to wait too long to introduce the conflict, the guts, the engine (as Sol Stein calls it), that element that makes the reader care and pulls her along. But stay out of the way of the fun of the story revealing itself to the reader. I even urge publishers to be careful not to give away too much of the story in what they call flap copy—the summary on the inside cover flaps designed to get you to buy the book. I'd rather see phrases like *She faces the toughest decision of her life* than *She has to decide whether to keep the child.* And *He finds himself almost unable* to go on after an unspeakable tragedy rather than He is suicidal after the murder of his wife.

Unless you're writing a thoroughgoing literary manuscript, avoid ten to twenty introductory pages of scene-setting, background, or history. That can all come out in the story. Don't delay the action. Get on with it.

The willing suspension of disbelief is in full force when we forget we're reading, when we are unaware we're turning pages, and when we let that cup grow cold. We're not reading; we're there. We're in the story. Can you imagine anything more gratifying to the writer?

I was once asked by a retail trade journal to write a piece about a day in the life of a book salesman, and I happened to choose a salesman who represented the company that had published my first novel, Margo. Margo could best be described as a mystery/romance, and the salesman I was chronicling was a fan of the book. I requested that, when he pitched Margo, he avoid mentioning that the author was sitting right there; I was to be introduced as what I was: a journalist on assignment. (I had also decided—in the name of objectivity and to avoid any appearance of a conflict of interest—not to mention my book in my article for the trade journal.)

Of course, my ears pricked up when he got to Margo during his first call. He and I sat in a cramped, cluttered office across from an overworked bookstore manager in the Midwest. The manager looked dubious when the salesman began raving about this small first novel, especially when he said, "It's so gripping that you can open it to any page and you'll want to read the next."

The manager seemed reluctant to accept an ARC (advance reader copy), but took it, opened it in the middle, and began to read silently. The salesman said, "I really think you'll find that this—" and the manager lifted his free hand for silence as he continued to read. I could have gone to heaven right then. I immediately regretted having insisted on anonymity.

I had already had an experience with *Margo* that was more encouraging than any sales report. I had finished the writing in the olden days before computers, and I carried my only copy of the manuscript with me on a flight to California. I was doing my final run through, tweaking it one more time before shipping it to the publisher.

When I finished the first half of the manuscript, I tucked those pages into the seat pocket in front of me and started on the last half. When I arrived at my hotel, I became just short of suicidal when I realized I had left that first half on the plane. I vowed never to eschew copy machines or carbon paper again, and began a series of frantic phone calls to the airline. After a sleepless night and another half day of torment, I got a call from a woman in the airline's lost-and-found department several states away.

"Tell me you found the first half of my manuscript," I said.

"I'll make you a deal," she said. "You send me the second half, and I'll send you the first." I tried to kiss her over the phone. I had grabbed and hooked a reader. Someone had willingly suspended disbelief.

Readers won't stay long with a story that rings false. If they're not ready to allow for a fourteen-year-old major leaguer, or to entertain the idea that a third of the U.S. population could instantaneously disappear right out of their clothes, or to imagine that Santa is real, your work is for naught. Your job is to write with such plausibility that they are eager to do their part, to uphold their end of the contract.

In the Lord of the Rings series, J.R.R. Tolkien crafts trolls, wizards, and monsters with such conviction that we accept the premise of a Middle Earth. We buy into these glorious fantasies central to the story. One of his techniques, crucial to any work of fiction, is to make sure that, in these otherwise unbelievable characters, the readers see something of themselves.

The tendril of faith that binds you to your reader is a fragile, sacred thing. Break it and the connection is lost.

One way to know whether you're on track is to evaluate the reactions from readers when a character dies. If you get despairing e-mails or letters or in-person comments, you've hooked them. You may think, *But it's fiction! The characters aren't real. Who cares? Get over it.*

On the contrary. If readers are upset at the death of a made-up person, you've done something right.

CLIFFHANGERS ALWAYS WORK

Or do they? I wrote a full-blown cliffhanger ending for *Assassins*, one of the Left Behind titles. The publishing house's marketing department loved it.

> Two hours before the burial, David Hassid was called in to Leon Fortunato's office. Leon and his directors of Intelligence and Security huddled before a TV monitor. Leon's face revealed abject grief and the promise of vengeance. "Once His Excellency is in the tomb," he said, his voice thick, "the world can approach closure. Prosecuting his murderer can only help. Watch with us, David. The primary angles were blocked, but look at this collateral view. Tell me if you see what we see."
>
> David watched.
>
> On, no! It couldn't be!
>
> "Well?" Leon said, peering at him. "Is there any doubt?"
>
> David stalled, but that only made the other two glance at him.
>
> "The camera doesn't lie," Leon said. "We have our assassin, don't we?"

> Much as he wanted to come up with some other explana-
> tion for what was clear, David would jeopardize his position if
> he proved illogical. He nodded. "We sure do."

And that was the end. Angry readers wrote that they had thrown the book across the room. It wasn't fair, they howled. Each book should be complete. Who was the assassin?

Maybe they were right. Perhaps I was needlessly tormenting them, seeming to force them to buy the next installment. I made sure the next book, *The Indwelling*, was self-contained. Wouldn't you know it, I got even more mail—from people saying they missed having a cliffhanger.

Let me toss in another *Assassins* story. I worked on that manuscript on airplanes as well, but kept the three-and-a-half-inch floppy disk on my person as a backup. (I now save my files, one per chapter, on my hard drive, back them up on a floppy, attach them to e-mails to my assistant—who also prints out a hard copy. See? I've learned.)

As is my custom, as I went through security at the airport, I had the manuscript disk in my pocket. Imagine the look on the guard's face when his wand detected something metallic and I produced a floppy disk labeled *Assassins*. When he demanded to know what that was about, I told him it was the next book in the Left Behind series, and found he was a fan.

"I may have to confiscate that," he said. "When does it come out?"

KEEPING YOUR PLOT FRESH

I've said that I am not an outliner, but before I wrote the first book in the Soon trilogy, I got cold feet. I knew it would be compared to the Left Behind books, and I wanted to ensure I had the safety net of a well-conceived plot. No simply putting interesting characters in interesting situations and seeing what happens, this time.

Even with that security, however, I found it difficult to write. I didn't leave myself enough rabbit trails to intuitively follow to let the story play out. The book sold well, and readers seemed to like it, but the writing experience left me frustrated.

With the second title, *Silenced*, I went back to my old, organic way of writing and felt much more comfortable. I like to be surprised, disappointed, or shocked along with the reader. As I write, anything I've ever experienced, read, seen, or even thought comes into play. I'm often shocked at where some of this stuff comes from—things from years past I didn't even know I had filed away in my brain.

Fiction has a mind of its own. It's organic. That makes me careful whenever I submit a novel proposal to a publisher. I feel obligated to say that I am not committing in advance to what they're reading. If the story heads another direction, I'm going to follow it and hope lots of readers do the same.

TELL A GOOD STORY

When readers can't put your book down, you've succeeded. Sometimes something as simple as parallel storylines with multiple perspective characters (making sure that you limit yourself to one point of view per scene, of course) will make the story sing and keep the pace moving.

In the Left Behind books, I switch back and forth between the perspectives of Rayford, the airline pilot, and Cameron (Buck) Williams, the globetrotting journalist. I write Rayford into a corner, putting him in a seemingly impossible situation, then simply leave an extra space and switch to Buck. Part of the reason I do this is that I don't know how Rayford will survive either, and if that uncertainty keeps my interest, I assume it will capture the reader's too. All the while I'm writing Buck into trouble, my subconscious is working on how to plausibly conjure an escape for Rayford.

Switching points of view keeps the storyline moving because readers—and I—want to know what happens next. I leave my characters in mini-cliffhanger situations from scene to scene and chapter to chapter. (I confess, it's a shameless marketing technique.)

I'm often asked how to plot a contemporary mainstream novel. My answer borrows liberally from Dean Koontz's masterpiece *How to Write Best-Selling Fiction*. He says to plunge your main character into terrible trouble as soon as possible, and be sure that everything he tries to do to escape just makes things worse and worse. When all seems lost, the character should have grown and learned enough to finally solve the problem himself.

If you think about it, I have just described the formula for every episode of *I Love Lucy*. Maybe Koontz's counsel resonates with me because I was raised on episodic TV sitcoms in the 1950s and 1960s. If your novel is boring you, start over with Koontz's formula in mind. It's not as simple as it looks (for instance, every new complication must logically arise from the actions of the protagonist to improve his situation), but it's a blueprint for success.

Q & A WITH JERRY

Do parables have a place in modern writing?

This reminds me of something I'm often asked: Should an inspirational writer, a person of faith, tell lies to convey truth? Honestly, I don't see a novel as a lie. Fiction is a vehicle to convey truth. So, yes. Jesus told the truth through parables.

With so many books in the Left Behind series, have you ever had a continuity problem, something inconsistent from one volume to another?

Sure. Readers have caught a few things. Tsion Ben-Judah initially had children young enough that they should have been Raptured. We fixed that in a reprint by making them stepchildren in their late teens.

I caught another mistake before it was published. One divine judgment temporarily diminishes the sun, which makes a huge difference in the temperature around the world. Subsequently, I have one of my main characters building a landing strip in the desert but wearing a sweater and long pants because of the decrease in temperature.

I put the temperature in the low sixties rather than in the normal low hundreds, and throughout the manuscript, carefully, consistently reinforced those details. Then it hit me: Hadn't that judgment already ended? I sped through the previous volume and, sure enough, that malady was over. I had to go back through my entire new manuscript and change all those particulars. Most readers would have caught that if my editors hadn't.

What do you say to those who have great novel ideas for you?

You've been reading my mail. While I appreciate the thought, I've got enough ideas of my own. I don't want anybody else's idea, in part because I don't want to be accused of stealing a story. Besides, half the fun of being a novelist is creating your own worlds.

Is co-authoring or collaborating difficult?

People always want to know how it works for Dr. LaHaye and me to co-write a book. The fact is, we don't. Left Behind was his idea, and he's the theological expert. I'm the novelist, and I do the writing.

It's been my experience, in both fiction and nonfiction, that collaboration works only if one person does all the writing. When I wrote as-told-to biographies, I made every effort to capture the phrasing and word choice of my subject so the text would sound like it was written by that person. Still, it remained my responsibility to do the writing.

I do collaborate on children's fiction now, working with my friend Chris Fabry. My own kids are all well past their teens now, but Chris and his wife have nine children, so he's up on the jargon and what's happening to kids the ages of our readers. We plot together, he does the writing, and I do the final edit and/or rewrite. Again, it works because there's one primary writer—Chris. If we were both trying to write, I can't imagine it working.

How do you know when a scene or chapter should end?

It's almost always earlier than you think. When I'm writing multiple-perspective narrative, I'll end a scene as powerfully as I can. The next day, I find there's at least one line before that break that I can still cut.

I'll say it again: Cutting nearly always improves the final product. Chop, chop, chop.

Writers write and write and write. Authors cut ~~and cut and cut~~.

Beginners often not only end scenes too late, they start scenes too early. If you merely edit your manuscript with this in mind—starting scenes later and ending them earlier—you'll punch up your story immeasurably. Start in the middle of action. Cut to the chase. You may have to go back and fill in a few transitions to make it make sense, but by then you're into the fun part: shaping. At every stage, think like a minimalist.

How do publishers select one novel proposal over another?

They're rightly trying to hedge their bets. Only one in ten new novels will be successful. Visibility is everything. Novelists who are known, even in a field or genre unrelated to their current project, have an advantage, fair or not. They have built-in audiences. But there are still publishing houses eager to give new authors a chance. They know word-of-mouth will build interest if a book proves worthy. Quality publishers take chances on new authors with promising skills and important messages.

Does every novel need romance?

I get tired of plots that include the generic beautiful woman. To my mind, that's the definition of gratuitous. I try to avoid that cliché. Often, romance seems right, because love relationships are so prevalent in real life. But still, you need to be careful of making your heroine a paper doll. You owe it to her—and to readers—to give her depth. Of course, the same is true about leading men.

How important is comic relief?

Every novel needs some. Even in the Left Behind series—which admittedly is about a very heavy subject—I try to introduce humor by taking shots at bureaucratic buffoons. We all enjoy watching someone, especially a villain, make a fool of herself. Breaks from the serious, especially in tragic stories, keep readers from getting depressed.

What are the most common plotting errors?

Predictability. I avoid main characters who can do no wrong. Heroes are nice, especially in kids' books. But we need to see their struggles too. They can still be heroes without being perfect. They can't be wimps or cowards or weaklings, but they can have real human flaws. Otherwise there can be no character arc, that growth so crucial to a satisfying story.

Villains have to be three-dimensional too. I'm not talking about making them sympathetic. They're the bad guys, after all. But they may have a soft side, a weak spot, even a certain generosity. And their evil has to have motivation. No one simply wears a black hat and is mean for no reason.

Another weakness in novels I review is dialogue, and this weakness has more to do with technique than plotting. As a novelist, you must take the time to listen to how people talk, and to make each character distinctive. The easiest trap to fall into is having everyone sound like you. Remember that real dialogue is repetitive and dull. So paraphrase. Help your characters get to the point.

Also, beginners need to strive to create plot twists that make sense. I like to be surprised when I'm reading, but not dumbfounded. You have to give readers enough hints that they can at least admit the groundwork was laid for a surprise. Readers love being let in on secrets and given clues, even if they don't figure the plot out in advance. But if the climax comes out of left field, your reader will feel betrayed.

Honor your contract with your reader. She'll willingly suspend disbelief if you play fair and give her a reason.

Have you ever wished you hadn't killed off a character?

Sure. I grow to love them as the readers do. After finding Pastor Barnes dead at the end of *Tribulation Force*, I sat back and said, "Wow, we've lost Bruce." Dr. LaHaye actually wanted him to come back to life in the next book, but I thought we had plenty of supernatural elements already. And anyway, the loss of the Tribulation Force leader forced me to create a new character to fill the bill.

OREL HERSHISER AND NOLAN RYAN

As a sports fan and then a sportswriter—but most importantly, as a father eager to pass along solid values to my sons—I have long been fascinated by what sets great athletes apart from superstars, and superstars from Hall of Famers. Several of my biography subjects have gone on to become Hall of Fame inductees in their respective sports, so I've been tempted to mention that as one of the perks of working with me—as if I had something to do with it.

Not every sports star I've written about is a person of faith, but most are, and all are good citizens, family people, people of character, people I would be proud to point my boys to as role models. In the process of working with so many over the years, I learned what sets apart the great ones.

World-class pros by definition have natural gifts, drive, and dedication. But they also have one other specific trait: an incredible competitive spirit, an addiction to competition. These people will compete at anything. They want to be the first done eating, the first through the door, first at everything. Whether playing a board game, pinball, racquetball, table tennis—any game, related to their profession or not—whether driving, arguing, or joking, they want to win.

That may also be true of you or people you know. It's not unusual to want to win. But with the Michael Jordans of this world, this competitive spirit manifests itself as an unbelievable, uncontrollable drive. I was discussing this one day with Orel Hershiser, then a pitcher for the Los Angeles Dodgers. Intriguing about Orel was that he didn't look the part of the spectacular athlete. He made fun of his own body. Tall and gangly, with a sunken chest and a pale boyish face, he looked more like a grown-up Opie than like a Bulldog, his nickname from manager Tommy Lasorda.

But I had noticed that Hershiser was ferociously devoted to his training regimen, and deceptively strong. He was good at a variety of sports and games. In relation to this, I said, "In fact, probably the only sport I could even compete with you at would be table tennis." I happened to be a tournament player and knew Orel to be a recreational player. Note that I didn't even claim I could beat him.

As the interview progressed and we moved on to other issues, his eyes kept dancing and he seemed preoccupied. I look for such clues to when a subject needs a break or a snack or to quit for the day. But that wasn't what was bothering Orel. He blurted, "Man, we've got to find a ping pong table." I should be glad we never found one. He might have schooled me in that sport as well.

As a lifelong baseball fan, I found it fascinating to spend time in a big league locker room, to be on the field before games, and to just soak up the milieu. I got to watch Orel warm up before a game, and it was hard to believe a human being could put such speed on a ball. He asked if I wanted to stand in the batter's box, not to hit but to just give him perspective.

I said, "No, I brought only one pair of pants."

Later he told me that the average adult male wouldn't be able to catch a big league fastball, let alone hit one. Of that I had no doubt, especially after standing within ten feet of his catcher while Orel was throwing ninety-two-mile-an-hour sinkers.

Nolan Ryan, the no-hit record holder and strikeout king, threw even harder. Watching him warm up his hundred-mile-an-hour fastball, even the smack in the catcher's glove was frightening. How batters stood in against that heat I'll never know.

And talk about competitive. I once watched Nolan pitch against his own wife in a family game at the ball park. I assumed he would lob in something the former softball player could easily get her bat on. But no. He was firing big league fastballs. To my amazement, and perhaps to his, Mrs. Ryan didn't strike out. In fact, she grounded a ball right back to him. If your spouse had just hit a ball your way, would you have missed the ball on purpose, or thrown it over the first baseman's head? Me too. Not Nolan. He made the play and threw her out.

That's competitive.

CHAPTER 10

Your Own Little World of Characters

I write what I like to read: stories with interesting characters in diffi-cult situations, stories full of tension and emotion. And I want to read those kinds of stories, and write them, from the first sentence of the first chapter. The opening of John Grisham's *The Testament* is a great example:

> Down to the last day, even the last hour now. I'm an old man,
> lonely and unloved, sick and hurting and tired of living. I am
> ready for the hereafter; it has to be better than this.

I was hooked, but that was the least of it. Within the next two pages, Grisham was speeding toward the dramatic conclusion to this riveting opening scene, which set the tone for the whole novel.

Daphne du Maurier's *Rebecca* begins: "Last night I dreamt I went to Manderley again." Provocative, lyrical, mysterious, and exotic. A clas-sic tale begun beautifully. In her dreams, the heroine returns to the lush estate she once shared with her husband, the site of a tragedy that might have been prevented had she only known then what she knows at the time of the story's narration. The opening lines of the novel perfectly capture the heroine's sense of loss and regret.

To succeed at fiction, we must create characters the reader cares about. Otherwise the action seems remote and pointless. If we do our jobs correctly, the reader gets caught in the middle of the action and *has* to find out what happens next. Is the car going off the cliff? Are the baby and its mother going to die? But even that kind of tension depends on getting the reader to care. No doubt you've been taught to begin at a high point of action, but don't forget to plant insights into the characters' personalities to make your reader sympathize.

Would you have cared about the old, suicidal man in the Grisham passage above if Grisham hadn't included the word *unloved*? We all know bitter old people, sick and hurting and dying, but unless we know them well, we care only as much as any thinking and feeling person might. Additional details evoke more empathy. If the person is a parent or grandparent or dear friend we once knew as a vital, loving, generous person, we care more. And our sympathy is aroused if we are clued in to the reason for the person's emotional unrest, like a feeling of being unloved. I don't know about you, but I was more intrigued by the Grisham character's sadness over that than by his thoughts of suicide. Once I grew to know him better, in just a few pages, I was genuinely intrigued by his plan to end his life. He was all the more interesting because he happened to be obscenely rich and was determined to thwart the family jackals monitoring his failing health. Grisham made me care about him.

Knowing when to let up on the action accelerator and slip in a few hints as to who the endangered person really is sets the pro apart from the amateur. The reader must soon get to know the person under fire in order to continue to willingly suspend disbelief. The more you can make readers care about the young mother and her baby, for example, the heavier the anxiety over their impending doom.

Although plunging mother and baby over a cliff makes for interesting reading, it's much more effective to allow the reader into their lives first. Is the mother thinking about the baby's first birthday party, planned for that evening, and hoping her husband has remembered? Has he been distant ever since the pregnancy, still tentative with the baby because they lost their first in childbirth?

Does she slowly, slowly, back out of the garage, checking every mirror twice or as many times as necessary, recalling a driveway tragedy from her childhood? All these thoughts foreshadow danger, but they also tell us about one of our protagonists. She's thoughtful, careful, loving, hopeful, worried.

Something should be riding on this birthday party. Maybe she thinks that, now that her daughter is a year old, her husband will return to his old self and she won't have to worry that someone at the office has caught his eye.

Now, when she absently allows herself to take a mountain curve too fast, and the car scrapes violently against the guardrail, and she catches a glimpse of the sheer drop-off, don't we care more than we might have if we'd simply started in the middle of that harrowing scene and stayed there, knowing nothing of the character's background?

Character is the foundation for fiction. Plot arises from quality characters. That's why the continuing series is so popular. I've heard from Left Behind readers who have caught themselves praying for the characters, or turning on CNN, thinking they're going to hear something about Nicolae Carpathia. That's when you know you've created characters people care about.

Your hero must be real, a normal man or woman who rises to the occasion. My characters say things I wish I would say, things that in real life I don't think of until it's too late. My characters learn to be direct and brave after having been tongue-tied and afraid. They change and grow. That's the definition of character arc.

Authors, too, must change and grow. If we are not different people by the end of the writing, something is wrong. And each effort should be an improvement over the last.

BIRTH OF A CHARACTER

One of my favorite memories is of a woman seeking me out in my office in Chicago. She was in her seventies, clad in black, way overdressed for the weather, bent, and dragging one foot.

"You the writer Jenkins?" she said.

"I am."

"Reader," she said. "Fan."

"Thanks."

"One question. Where do you get your ideas for characters?"

What could I say—*From people like you*? I said, "I make 'em up."

"Figured as much. Good day."

The truth is, while many ideas come simply from seeing people like her and imagining what their lives must be like, characters appear in my mind's eye as I'm writing. The more vital the character is to the story, the more clearly I see him.

Some characters are furniture, utilitarian, just there to move the action. Even in those cases, however, I always appreciate a writer who eschews central casting and offers something interesting. I don't want every cop to be Irish. I don't want every coroner to be Asian. I don't want every bar tender to be laconic and bored.

You don't even have to name orbital characters, but they should be interesting. In *The Operative*, my lead buys a gun on the black market in South America from a national wearing thick, black, horn-rimmed glasses. That's all we know about him. My guess is you already have a picture of him in your mind. You see him a certain height, have given him a hair color, can probably even hear his accent.

I want you to see him your way, fat and dumpy or tall and thin. My only detail is his eyewear. And the second time I refer to him, I call him Glasses. I've referred to others as Big Mouth, Pants, or Shoes. I don't need you to get to know them; they're just props. But, I hope, distinctive ones.

Some may disagree with me when I say you don't need to have developed your entire cast of characters when you start a novel. But I still think it's far more fun for you and the reader if you put your lead characters together and see who shows up at the door. In the Margo mysteries, I introduced a big detective who proved earthy and likeable. Readers (and I) fell in love with him. Eventually he took over the series.

The more important a character is, the better you should know his personality. His physical description, however, can be left much to the reader's imagination. I like to offer hints, but that's all. Other writers are gifted at describing people. If you are, run with it. But remember that readers often enjoy seeing a character they way he looks in their own minds. Here are a few tips for creating memorable characters.

Let 'em talk. Characters often reveal themselves in what they say, and they can—and should—surprise even you. I've tried to force words into their mouths, only to have them shake their fists at me and say what they want. When a character comes out with some shocking pronouncement, you should ask, "What do you mean?" The serendipitous story—within reason (you should always be prepared to backtrack when a rabbit trail leads nowhere)—can be as delightful to the reader as it is to you.

No twins allowed. As a reader, I appreciate it when the storyteller clearly distinguishes each character. I don't even want two characters to have similar names, unless that is important to the plot. Don't make your reader wonder whom you're writing about. Give characters distinct names, clear voices, different mannerisms.

Characterize with dialogue and dialect. Use dialect sparingly. It's difficult to read, and a little goes a long way. Have a character say *gonna* for *going to* only once or twice, and the reader will hear it that way from then on.

I don't pretend that every character is educated and articulate. Readers know better. And you can hint at distinct speech patterns merely by word choice and order:

"He say he gonna get me if I tell a soul what he done."

"I beg your pardon? This man threatened you?"

You don't have to be a genius to tell those two characters apart, and I didn't have to riddle the page with apostrophes and misspellings to render the dialect of the less educated one.

Play tag. Because you don't want every character in your novel to be quirky, give them tags so readers can tell them apart. Some should use contractions and some shouldn't. Some will be heady, some airy, and others terse, or earthy. Give them little visual tags as well. Maybe one smokes, another wears glasses that slide down her nose, and another is always manicured.

Make them real. Remember, heroes need weaknesses, but not weaknesses that repulse the reader. You can have a private eye who's afraid of the dark, but he shouldn't be a bed-wetter. A lead female character can talk too much or too fast, but she can't be a coward or a crybaby.

Their histories make your heroes who they are. Did he have a terrifying experience with insects as a child, which makes him kill every bug he sees? Was she abandoned by her father, which makes her distrust men who claim to care for her?

Challenge your characters. Force your characters out of their comfort zones. In the Left Behind series my globetrotting journalist, Buck, kills a man attempting to foil his escape. He didn't want to, didn't mean to. But either Buck disarms the guy or he and his loved ones are captured. Naturally, I had to then examine his response to the death. If he had been a commando raider, he wouldn't have given it a second thought. It was kill or be killed. But Buck is more like you or me. He was forced to do something hellacious, and now he has to live with it.

Create the ultimate villain. Your villain must have reasons for being rotten, or your readers won't buy him. And your bad guy shouldn't always look like one. He is who he is because he is jealous, has been abused, is angry, was jilted, was swindled, or feels inferior because of his social or educational status. Don't put him on the page until you've concocted that motivation.

I create bad guys by looking within. I'd like to think few people see me as a villain, but often the best way to find dark motivation is to admit your own darkness. We can all be nasty. Do you lash out from behind the wheel, saying things you're glad no one else hears? Do you shake your fist or your finger at someone, then panic to think it might be someone you know? What drove you to such rage? What might make your villain so cruel?

Using the antichrist—evil by definition—as a villain in the Left Behind series was not as easy as it might seem. Motivation was no problem. He wanted to be above God. Unbridled pride got him cast out of heaven. Making him believable as a human being was the tough part. Billions fall for the greatest con man of the ages. What would convince the world he was not their enemy but their savior?

Most fascinating is that biblical prophecy says the antichrist will be so attractive and popular that nearly everyone will believe not only that he is not evil, but that he is God incarnate. In a human sense, Nicolae Carpathia appears to be the greatest mortal who ever lived. Whereas Scripture says Jesus was "of no form nor comeliness that we should desire him," the antichrist is compared to an angel of light. I portray him as a young Robert Redford, an impeccable dresser, someone who speaks eight languages fluently. In *Left Behind*, Nicolae, without notes, recounts the history of the U.N., lists every member nation, is revered by all, and sways everyone he speaks to. Readers are swept along with the rest of his fans.

My son Chad was eighteen when he read the manuscript, and halfway through, he said, "I hope this Carpathia guy isn't the antichrist, because I really like him."

Some readers missed the point. They suggested Christopher Walken or John Malkovich to play Carpathia in a movie. Those happen to be two of my favorite actors, but who would they fool? Who would be deceived into thinking they were good guys until they showed their true colors?

In many stories, it's effective to hide the true villain until the moment of truth. In *The Operative*, one of the friendliest, most folksy and sympathetic characters turns out to be the culprit.

Keep track. Writing out a character sketch—even a short bio—can help keep you straight, but don't feel obligated to use every tidbit of someone's history. That background informs your writing, helps you understand the character. Tell the reader only what he needs to know to understand.

I create a sheet as I write that reminds me who is where. You need a handle on where your characters are, but beware the amateurish tendency to report on the location and activity of everyone in every scene, especially if these details add nothing to the story. I've seen beginners set a scene by telling where everyone in the family was. Why not just say, "Sarah arrived home to find her mother alone"? Unless it's important where everyone else is, why do we care?

Avoid the name game. Unless you're writing a fable or a parable or a bodice ripper, use restraint. I don't like names you'd find only in a novel: Crest Weatherstone. Raven Blaze. Troy Hawk. I'm not advocating Mary Smith and Jim Anderson. Character names should have a little music, but be careful not to make them so obscure or ethnic that they distract.

On the other hand, in my Christmas fantasy *'Twas the Night Before*, it made sense to use some names with clear double meanings. The annoying, needling guy no one can stand? Gary Noyer.

The main character, a Doubting Thomas? Tom Douten.

And the other lead, the pure-hearted adult who still literally believes in Santa and is Tom's Miss Right? Noella Wright.

For mainstream fiction, I try to choose interesting, somewhat unusual names, and these are found everywhere. A woman in a commercial named Jae. Another named Cydia.

Be careful of kids' names, because their popularity changes over the years. You don't want an Ethel or a Myrtle unless your story is set in the early twentieth century, or unless that unfortunately anachronistic moniker is an element of the story.

I came up with Nicolae Carpathia because Nicolae is the most common surname in Romania, and the Carpathian Mountains are the most prominent there. A reader told me that naming a Romanian character Nicolae Carpathia was akin to naming an American character Joe Mountain.

For many characters, I use names of people I know, borrowing a first name from one and a last name from another. I use one friend's gender, another's looks, another's mannerisms. I have friends named Dean and Grace; in the Soon series, I name a character Grace Dean. In the Left Behind series, Steve Plank is named after an old friend, Steve Board.

Don't overstate spirituality. One of the thorniest problems with inspirational fiction is that the spiritual part gets clunky. We authors too often feel obligated to say things certain ways. But a character's spirituality is best woven into the fabric of his personality.

Allow me to exaggerate here to make the point: Your main character performs a selfless, perhaps even sacrificial, act. Maybe she takes the blame for something someone else did, to save that person the embarrassment. Or maybe she actually takes that person's punishment. That is so clearly a Christ-like act that you must avoid the temptation to explain it as such, or worse, have the character explain it as such.

Let's take it a step further and say that the main character shows a willingness to give her very life for someone else.

> "You pushed the little girl from in front of the train, Margaret, but you lost your legs in the process. What made you do it?"
> "Well, I could do no less, since I have been redeemed by the precious blood of the Lamb who gave Himself for me on the cross."

Now, I hesitate to make light of beautiful word pictures that mean everything to believers, but you can see how plainly clunky and unrealistic that dialogue is. The woman did this because she's the heroine, and because the act exhibited a willingness to die—if necessary—in someone else's stead; it need not be explained. Give the reader credit. He gets it.

WRITING FOR THE SOUL

You must also resist the implication that only a Christian—who believes Jesus died for her—would perform such an act. Some people are simply brave and will do the right thing, regardless of their personal beliefs. The parallel between what they have done and what we Christians believe Jesus did for us is still clear. And examining the thorny implications of a non-Christian performing such a Christ-like act can provide a hundred pages of most interesting fiction.

In the movie *Tender Mercies*, the character Mac Sledge (played by Robert Duvall) becomes a Christian believer. He doesn't become one who begins spouting spiritual platitudes. He simply becomes a more contemplative, loving, peaceful person. His new faith becomes part of his character, and it works.

In *Hometown Legend*, there was no need for fanfare before talking about God. One of the main characters, Rachel Sawyer, prays in the first scene. It was a natural part of her life.

Later, when the head coach gathers the team around him before the big game, he says, "Supreme Court or not, I'm praying." We don't then show the actual prayer, but that expression alone resulted in cheers from the audience at almost every showing.

Surprise, surprise. One of the reasons I wanted to get into fiction in the first place was my frustration with real-life subjects. Oh, they were interesting enough, but often I thought, *If he had taken the other path at this crossroad, it would have been much more dramatic.* My thought was that, when I finally wrote a novel, I'd decide which road the character took.

Surprise. Fictional characters can be every bit as cantankerous as real people. You can't make them do what they don't want to do. Trust your characters, follow them, let them show you the story.

I like to put characters together and see what happens. Often I think a couple is destined to fall in love, only to find that they can't stand each other, and that another unlikely tryst arises.

Almost every conversation in a novel should be an argument, or reveal deceit, or show tension. If you're not advancing the plot with riveting dialogue, you're better off paraphrasing. During the rewrite, I chop dialogue to its essence. No one wants to hear characters greet each other and trade pleasantries. Summarize that part and get on with it: "After they greeted each other, Jane said, 'I assume you've heard the news.'"

My characters all tend to sound like me in the first draft. Man or woman, old or young, they sound like Jerry. As I edit, I chop off the beginnings of most spoken sentences. "Do you think you're going to want lunch at noon?" becomes "Want lunch at noon?" That's how people talk. More literary types use more complete sentences. Remember, every character needs his own voice.

MADELINE MANNING

A unique opportunity came my way in the mid-1970s, when Word Books asked me to write the autobiography of Cleveland-born Olympic runner Madeline Manning (now Mims). She was an African-American Christian and single mom, and she was the first world-class American woman in the 800-meter run. She was a world-record holder, and won the gold medal in the event at the 1968 Olympics in Mexico City. She retired from competition in 1970, but returned in 1972 for the Munich games. After losing in the Olympic 800-meter semifinals of the 800-meter, she won a silver on the 400-meter relay team.

Madeline retired again once more after the 1972 Olympics, but began competing again in 1975. She became the first American woman to break two minutes in the 800-meter, running a 1:59.8 at the 1976 Olympic trials.

Madeline felt God had called her to run in the Olympics in Montreal in 1976, and that He had told her she would shine there.

My job was to tell her story, the tale of an unlikely comeback Olympic winner.

The night before I was to go to Montreal to watch her run for the gold, I sat home watching her in the qualifying heat on television. She finished dead last. Eighth out of eight. Of course she did not qualify for the finals.

Was there still a story? Would she want to see me, let alone talk to me? What would this mean for the book? My ticket was nonrefundable, and if I had learned anything about world-class athletes, it was that they faced their failures as grown-ups. I went to Montreal.

By the time I met with her, Madeline was over it. She was bubbly and excited. Oh, she had had her explosion. She had raged and cried and wondered what she was to think of her conviction that God had told her she would shine.

Why had she lost the semifinal? She had, she realized, made a tactical error. While watching that first semifinal, she imagined herself in it. As the runners circled the 400-meter oval twice, Madeline mentally jockeyed for position, waited to make her move, then saw herself bursting past everyone for the win. She believed her body released chemicals that would have allowed her to run that first race well. But the visualization drained her, and she was spent before it was actually her turn in the second race. Lactic acid had built up in her muscles. And she was in oxygen debt.

It was a huge error, especially for someone who should have known better. But Madeline wasn't alone in her loss. For whatever reason, many American athletes who had been favored to win medals that year lost by hundredths of a second. These suffering athletes came away hurt, angry, and depressed. And they looked for their mentor, the elder stateswoman, their spiritual leader.

By that time, Madeline believed God had revealed to her what His promise had meant. A light doesn't shine as brightly when seen from the mountaintop of victory. It is most effective illuminating in an otherwise dark valley, and that is where Madeline had found herself. Finally coming to terms with her role, and having dealt with the disappointment of having coming out of retirement and returning to world-class form only to lose, she set about counseling her teammates. Madeline came to believe she had been called to suffer in order to help others.

Frankly, that made for a better book too. It was called *Running for Jesus*.

CHAPTER 11

Your Perspective Party

Your choice of point of view can make or break your short story or novel.

Imagine your story as a party with you as host. You've invited old friends, new friends, neighbors, and acquaintances. Your job is to choreograph the events so people feel comfortable and never wonder what's going on.

You greet guests at the door and introduce them to each other, get conversations started. Without being intrusive, your aim is to make sure everyone has a good time.

We've all been to parties where the host has not covered the basics. Although we don't expect our host to be the center of attention, we expect her to manage the details. When this is done right, we hardly notice. We simply know we've had a good time. When details are neglected, everyone leaves with a bad taste.

Picture yourself as the host of your fiction party. Invite readers to a treat. Don't take center stage, but manage the basics in such a way that the reader barely notices. Nothing should jar her as she engages with your characters and plot.

No one should notice that you followed the rules of perspective, that you limited your point of view to one character per scene. But they'll notice if you don't.

In my more than seventy novels, I've written in first-person, third-person, and omniscient points of view. There are many options: first person (singular or plural), second person, third person (single, multiple, subjective, and objective), and omniscient.

Regardless which you choose, there is one unbreakable rule: one perspective, one point of view per scene.

When you violate this cardinal rule, few readers (unless they study writing) will think, *Hey, she switched perspective characters on me!* But they will feel like the underdressed partygoer, standing awkwardly in the middle of the room, not knowing what to do.

Veteran editor Dave Lambert, formerly of HarperCollins-Zondervan, says, "No decision you make in writing a story will have more impact on its shape and texture than your choice of point of view."

William Sloane, in *The Craft of Writing*, says, "In the best fiction and most of the time, the reader is identifying with one or another of the characters.... He is *being* the Ishmael of *Moby Dick*. He is *being* the narrator of *Deliverance*. He is not, be it noted, being either Herman Melville or James Dickey."

In Stephen King's *The Green Mile*, the story is told by the man in charge of death row, the role played by Tom Hanks in the movie version. His primary role is to get prisoners to the electric chair at the appointed hour. We meet everyone waiting for execution, including a man with strange powers. The storyteller tries to give the ultimate down-and-outers dignity during their last hours. He also is the one most deeply impacted by the strange prisoner. It makes sense that

Internal Dialogue

Getting inside a person's head is fun. Imagine a character thinking, *I hate that guy and always have. He ripped me off, stole my wife, and crashed my car.*

Now put him in a scene with his nemesis and have him say, "Good to see you again, Phil. I'm looking forward to working together." When Phil responds positively, the reader knows someone's lying. Probably both of them. Continue that way throughout your story, and the reader will wonder to the end who is being real and who is not.

we hear the tale from his perspective. Always choose as your point-of-view character the one with the most as stake. If you use multiple characters, choose the one with the most at stake in the given scene.

SET UP THE FIRST SCENE

My challenge in writing the Left Behind series is the scope of the narrative. It is of biblical proportions and is set not only all over the globe, but also occasionally in the heavens. It's the ultimate story of the battle between good and evil, heaven and hell.

When my agent shopped the first ten-page chapter of the first book, it contained one scene, written from the perspective of the pilot of a 747. In the middle of the night, over the Atlantic, about a third of his passengers disappear right out of their clothes, leaving everything material behind.

That's enough drama to engage the reader, but I knew the main character had to be someone real and human, easily identified with. Otherwise, the story could spiral into merely a plot-driven thriller.

So I began:

> Rayford Steele's mind was on a woman he had never touched. With his fully loaded 747 on autopilot above the Atlantic en route to a 6 A.M. landing at Heathrow, Rayford had pushed from his mind thoughts of his family.
>
> Over spring break he would spend time with his wife and twelve-year-old son. Their daughter would be home from college, too. But for now, with his first officer dozing, Rayford imagined Hattie Durham's smile and looked forward to their next meeting.
>
> Hattie was Rayford's senior flight attendant. He hadn't seen her in more than an hour.

From the first phrase, I wanted the readers in the main character's mind. Then, in short order, they learn his line of work and where he is. They soon discover he's a married family man tempted to stray.

After a few pages to set the scene, Rayford yields to the urge to see his love interest right then.

> As he opened the cockpit door, Hattie Durham nearly bowled him over....
>
> The senior flight attendant pulled him into the galley way, but there was no passion in her touch. Her fingers felt like talons on his forearm, and her body shuddered in the darkness....
>
> "People are missing," she managed in a whisper, burying her head in his chest.
>
> He took her shoulders and tried to push her back, but she fought to stay close. "What do you m—"
>
> She was sobbing now, her body out of control. "A whole bunch of people, just gone!"

I was tempted, of course, to switch to Hattie's perspective. She was the one in crisis, terrified, living a nightmare. It would have been easy and might even have seemed natural to say, "Hattie was scared to death by what she had just seen." But not only would this violation of the show-don't-tell rule have been clichéd, it would have ridden roughshod over the one-perspective-per scene principle.

When writers jump from brain to brain within the same scene, that's called omniscient viewpoint, an archaic approach that is also confusing, amateurish, and a mistake. *Didn't Dickens do that?* you say. Yes. More than a hundred years ago. It doesn't work anymore.

Notice how everything we know about Hattie comes from Rayford's perspective: He's nearly bowled over, he's pulled with talon-like fingers, he feels her shudder, he hears her speak.

MAKE CLEAN SWITCHES

That chapter sparked publishers' interest, and soon five publishers made offers. Tyndale House won the contract, and then it was put-up-or-shut-up time for me. No one had an inkling *Left Behind* would become a publishing phenomenon, but it was clear Tyndale was excited about it and had big expectations for the manuscript.

I had a nagging feeling. I felt positive about the sample chapter—how the scene had been set and the main perspective character established. But the story I wanted to tell was so big, I needed another perspective character, someone who could be where Rayford Steele couldn't be.

While Rayford was home with his daughter or getting back to flying when the air routes were reopened, someone had to be globe-trotting. I needed a pair of eyes in New York, then London, then Israel. It was too much to expect of a pilot without turning him into a comic book hero.

When I began to write in earnest, I used that first sample chapter as a framework, but I interrupted it right in the middle. While Rayford is still trying to talk himself into seeing Hattie, we move from the cockpit to first class. And to be sure to keep the reader with me, to show a shift not only in setting but in perspective, I inserted an extra line space and even added a horizontal line. (A mere double space indicates only a shift in time or location. The reader may assume the main character is still the narrator, even in third person.)

There's no secret to changing perspective characters. You must be clear and courteous to the reader, just as you would be to a guest. I wanted to leave zero doubt in the reader's mind what was going on. The last thing I wanted was for her to shake her head and say, "What is this, now?"

Plenty of secrets can be fairly kept from the reader. Sometimes she can tell a character is lying when the perspective character can't, and she knows something's going on. But you don't want her confused about who's telling the story.

My solution in *Left Behind*, besides the obvious space and line, was to immediately establish the new perspective character:

> Next to a window in first class, a writer sat hunched over his laptop.... At thirty, Cameron Williams was the youngest ever senior writer for the prestigious *Global Weekly*....

From this point on, Cameron (Buck) will share the point-of-view load. Until book five in the series, he and Rayford are the only two perspective characters. We go only where they go, hear their thoughts, see what they see. And every time the story switches from one to the other, I made sure to give the reader clear clues.

After several pages establishing Cameron and foreshadowing how events will affect him, I switched back to Rayford with a space and a line. But I wanted it even more obvious than that:

> Not sure whether he'd follow through with anything overt, Captain Rayford Steele felt an irresistible urge to see Hattie Durham right then.

The above reminds the reader of Rayford's internal struggle, but just to be sure the readers could follow the change in perspective, I reverted to whole names again for both him and Hattie. I didn't want my guests wondering what was going on.

USE SOLID SIGNALS

Chapter two of *Left Behind* starts with Cameron. Again, because it was early in the book and I was determined to clearly establish two separate characters, I used his full name: "Cameron Williams had roused when …"

A few pages later, the reader is back with Rayford.

> The first officer had been gone only a few minutes when Rayford heard his key in the cockpit door and it banged open.

By letting the readers hear what Rayford heard, I subtly told them I had left Williams, and that Steele had become their eyes and ears again.

By book five in the series (which will eventually comprise sixteen titles), it had become obvious that the story needed even more perspective characters. Minor and orbital characters became more prominent, and when the reader needed to know what was going on with them while Rayford and Cameron were otherwise engaged, I merely added my space and line and clearly introduced the new point-of-view character:

> Just after dark in New Babylon, David took a call from his routing manager....

Often, changing perspectives allows you to also make plain a change in location:

> Mac delicately lowered the skids onto the pavement at the east side of the hangar that housed the Condor 216.

You can also accomplish a time shift along with a perspective change:

> David Hassid walked Mac McCullum back to his quarters in the GC palace residential annex late that night.

Using multiple perspective characters proved an effective tool in telling my story. It will work for you too. Just remember that bouncing in and out of the head of more than one character per scene will make your reader feel like a neglected party guest, wondering what's going on.

A gracious writer will invite guests in, make everything clear, then get out of the way and let the fun begin. Resolve to send readers home from your fiction party eager to return.

PAUL ANDERSON

Once you start becoming known for a certain type of project, publishers may start coming to you with ideas. That's a free-lancer's dream, of course, and I learned to never say no. There's so much competition out there that if you don't want to write something, someone else certainly will.

Just after my Hank Aaron, Pat Williams, and Dick Motta books were released, Victor Books asked if I would write an autobiography for Paul Anderson, the world's strongest man. I had seen Anderson featured on television and in a documentary, and I had read some articles about him. I couldn't wait to meet him.

The 1956 Olympic gold medal winner for power lifting, Anderson ran a boys' home in Vidalia, Georgia, and raised funds for it by traveling and speaking and performing unbelievable feats of strength. He was listed in Guinness World Records for the most amount of weight ever hoisted by a human (6,270 pounds in a back lift in 1957).

Anderson was five-foot-nine and weighed 375 pounds. And he had a voice as big as his body. Even in normal conversation, his voice boomed. Paul was an amazing athlete for a guy who looked like a walking fire hydrant. He showed me the billiards room at the boys' home, and as we stood chatting, he went into a deep knee squat, then thrust himself into the air and alighted on the pool table like a cat. My mouth dropped open. The boys, apparently used to this, yawned.

Anderson could do something back then, in the 1970s, that no one else in the world could do. Only a few can match it today. He could do a clean-and-jerk—a move in which the lifter pulls the bar from the floor to his chest, settles, then drives it over his head—of nearly six hundred pounds.

I wanted a picture of him doing that.

Paul had the boys bring out his bar and the iron disk bells and set up the massive piece of apparatus. Meanwhile, he stretched and warmed up, and was clearly preparing mentally. He was about to perform an astounding feat for just me and a few of the teen boys.

He lifted the bar with a great grunt, settled, then fired it overhead. I shot the picture, he dropped the bar, and I said, "I was sort of hoping to get several different angles."

And there came that huge voice. "Well, you don't just hold six hundred pounds over your head all day, you know."

I could see the wisdom of that.

But he told me he had a set of phony disks, made of wood and painted black, that looked just like the iron ones. If I wanted, he would have the boys change them out, and I could shoot him lifting what looked like the same apparatus, except that he could hold it overhead as long as I needed. I was dubious until I saw the disks. I knew they would fool the camera. I assumed the wood was balsa. Seeing Anderson sweat with the phony weights aloft should have been a clue to their true weight, but I wasn't thinking. I got all my shots as well as an idea: Wouldn't my wife love a picture of me with what looked like six hundred pounds over my head?

Anderson agreed to trade places. I would lift. He would shoot.

We have the world's first photographically recorded attempt at a double hernia. The phony weights weighed 275 pounds. I got those babies about an inch off the ground, and the picture shows me with big eyes and the color drained from my face.

And I was right. Dianna loved that picture.

Paul Anderson, who died in 1994, was a man of faith, popular for telling crowds, "I'm the strongest man in the world, and if I can't get through one day without Jesus Christ, what about you?"

He was also a stickler about foul language. None of the boys in his home were allowed to swear, and if they did, there was, well, heck to pay.

The day he drove me back to the airport, we were waiting for my plane, and a man with his back to us was frustrated about something and said, "Jesus Christ!"

Anderson bristled and stared, and when the man said it again, Paul rushed him from behind, wrapped those tree trunk arms around his waist, and lifted him off the ground. "Where is He?" Paul said. "He's a friend of mine!"

The guy peeked over his shoulder and saw this mountain of a man and said, "Oh, my God!"

Anderson said, "That's Him! Where is He?"

I thought the guy was going to wet his pants. And I dare say he never swore again without first looking over his shoulder.

CHAPTER 12

Thickening the Stew

CLICHÉS AND CLUTTER

The morning-routine cliché. You don't likely need me to tell you what a cliché is, but you may be surprised to know that clichés come in all shapes and sizes. There are just as many clichéd scenes as phrases and words. For instance, how may times have you seen a book begin with a main character being "rudely awakened" from a "sound sleep" by a "clanging alarm clock"? Have you written an opening like this yourself? Wondering where to start, you opt for first thing in the morning. Speaking of clichés, been there, done that. We all have. Don't ever do it again.

Compounding that cliché is having the "bleary-eyed" character drag himself from his bed, squinting against the intruding sunlight. And compounding *that* is telling the reader everything the character sees in the room. What comes next? He will pass by or stand before a full-length mirror, and we'll get the full rundown of what the poor guy looks like.

Are you cringing? I've done the same kind of clichéd scene. Resolve to leave that whole morning-routine cliché to the millions of writers who will follow in your footsteps.

I know you want me to suggest alternatives to those hackneyed constructs, but inventing fresh ways to start a story and describe a character is your job. If an early morning routine is endemic to your plot—say your character is wound tight and sleepless because of a crucial morning meeting—put him on the commuter train with an unsupervised child darting about. He doesn't know what she's doing amidst all the businesspeople, with their noses stuck in newspapers or laptop screens, but she points at him and says, "Don't you comb your hair?"

Mortal dread. Is it possible that, in his hurry to catch the last train that would get him to his job interview on time, our hero actually skipped a step in his personal toilet? Now he has to find his reflection in the train window or the aluminum back of the seat in front of him. And then what does he do?

The answering-the-phone cliché. Another deadly cliché is how people answer the phone. This happens even in the movies or on stage. Be aware of yourself the next time your phone rings. It's such a common occurrence that we don't even think about it. But one thing you likely do *not* do is look up, startled. You don't turn and look at the phone. You know where it is; it's been there for years, and you've heard it ring before. You simply rise and go answer it.

If your character gets a phone call, resist the urge to have her look up, startled, then rise, cross the room, pick up the receiver, and say, "Hello?"

"Hi, Mary?"

"Yes."

"This is Jill."

"Hi, Jill. What's up?"

(Or, if you're a mystery writer) "Hi, Jill. Is anything wrong?"

Enough already.

The clutter of detail. Here's another problematic phone scene, from an unpublished manuscript:

> The tinny ring echoed through the dark house. The shiny white receiver waited on the stone countertop. Another outburst. Chester, handsome, dark-haired, and taller than normal, craned his neck to look at the ringing reminder of his loneliness. After the phone's third cry for attention, Chet stood up and strode purposefully toward the kitchen. His long legs were encased in brown corduroys, which swished in the silence as he moved toward the phone. Ring four. He knew the machine would click on if he didn't move quickly. He plucked the receiver delicately from the cradle with his bronzed hand and said in warm, resonant tones, "Hello. Chester here."
>
> "Hi, Chester. It's Mary."

You get the idea. Here's my version:

> Late that night, Mary phoned.

Give the readers credit. If you tell them Mary phoned Chester, they can assume Chester heard the ring, stood, moved to the phone, picked it up, and introduced himself. You'd be amazed at how many manuscripts are cluttered with such details.

Even in a period piece in which the baking of a cake from scratch is an engrossing trip down memory lane, the good writer gives readers credit for thinking. While she may outline all the steps the heroine goes through to make the cake, she will avoid having her rise and stride to the kitchen or even pull open the oven door—unless there's something about that oven door novel enough to include. If the character has to use a towel to lift the iron lid, fine. But if she does that, we know she had to stand and walk first.

Skip the recitals of ordinary life. We all get dressed, walk out to the car, open the door, slide in, turn the key, and back out of the driveway. If your character backs into the garbage truck, that's a story. Just say it:

> That morning, as Bill backed out of the driveway, his mind was on the tongue-lashing he had endured the day before from his boss. Only when he heard the ugly crunch and scrape and his head snapped back did he realize he had not bothered to check his rearview mirror. He had plowed into a garbage truck that looked half as big as his house.

Dialogue. One of the clichés of conversation is feeling the need to explain more than once what's going on, as if the reader can't figure it out on his own. I actually read a novel in which, when a character said something quirky like "Promptly, punctually, and prissily" (which was actually funny and fit the personality), the author felt the need to add, "he said alliteratively." Sure glad that was clarified.

Other writers have a character respond to a diatribe from another with "Yep," or "Nope," or a shrug. Perfect. I love to learn about personalities this way. The character is a man of few words. But too often, the author intrudes, adding, "he said, eschewing small talk." Yeah, we got that.

If you create a character who backs into a conversation with tentative phrases like "'Oh, I was just wondering'" or "'I don't know how to say this, but if I, well, let me say it this way'" we get it. We understand this is a timid, nervous person, afraid of saying something wrong, sensitive to others' feelings. Avoid the temptation to explain. Don't follow that with, "she began nervously, unsure how to broach the subject."

Maybe the responder to that speaker says, "'Is there a question in there somewhere? What *are* you saying?'" That tells us all we need to know. You don't have to explain with, "the insensitive jerk said."

Listen to people express themselves. Note cultural similarities and distinctive characteristics. Is the husband an old-school patriarch, or henpecked? See how the subjects behave differently based on how comfortable they are expressing themselves or sharing family secrets. Television documentaries capture foreign dialogue, showing how people of other cultures speak. The mall, church, a public gathering—all can become your listening and evaluating laboratories.

My favorite advancement in the writing of dialogue—though I admit it is slow in taking hold—is the realization that the word *asked* is almost always redundant: "'Where's the dog?' he asked." The sentence of dialogue is interrogative, and it ends with a question mark. Is it not redundant to add "he asked"? I never use *asked* in attributions any more: "'Where's the dog?' he said."

That's all you need. Yes, it occasionally jars readers. Sometimes editors will even start changing *said* back to *ask* until they realize I've been so consistent with it that it must be on purpose. More and more writers are replacing *ask* with *said*, and to me it only makes sense.

As you rewrite and polish, read your dialogue aloud and listen for problems with cadence. Your editor—and your reader—will be glad you did.

THEME

One thing I'll never be mistaken for is a literary writer. When I am criticized, it is for pedestrian writing. Well, I am pedestrian, and I write for the pedestrian reader. If I were more intelligent, perhaps my writing would be deeper.

I say this to clarify that when I discuss theme, I am not talking about the cosmic, overarching, universal, symbolic metaphors that might be found in literary novels. But even mainstream fiction must have a theme. And in my mind, it should be clear to the average reader.

For example, in *Though None Go With Me*, my theme was the cost of true devotion to God. My main character is a woman born in 1900 who grows up with the twentieth century. In her early teens, she makes a decision to make the rest of her life an experiment in obedience to God.

Almost instantly she becomes a female Job, and her commitment affects her entire life. Anything that can go wrong, does. The questions become: *Will she remain true to God? Is it worth it? Is there any payoff for that kind of a life, this side of heaven?*

If your whole reason for writing is to pontificate on, for example, the dangers of certain habits or lifestyles, you risk sounding preachy. I see this problem in many manuscripts: all talk, straw men, plots contrived to prove a point, but little that grabs and subtly persuades the reader. If your theme is the danger of alcoholism, simply tell a story in which an alcoholic suffers because of his bad decisions, and give the reader credit. Trust me, he'll get it. If your story is powerful enough, your theme will come through.

As you might imagine, preachiness is the bane of too much writing today, especially in the inspirational market. We are trying to make the same kinds of points, naturally, that preachers do. But preachers are *supposed* to preach. It's what they do. No one complains that his preacher is too preachy. That would be like saying a ballerina is too dancey.

For some reason, however, preachiness on paper offends the reader's sensibilities. If you're like me, you like to be given some credit as a reader and thinker. Even as a child, when I heard the story of the boy who cried wolf, I got it. I didn't need someone saying, "So you see, Jerry, if you lie often enough, no one will take you seriously when you're telling the truth." That's the beauty of morality tales. They make their own points.

Preachiness does not need to be as obvious as stopping the story to say, "And so, dear reader, as you travel down life's highway, remember ..." Sometimes obvious point-making comes when the writer of a first-person piece tries to shift gears without engaging the clutch, and writes, "That was the day I learned that if that little girl could be so brave in the face of that kind of danger, I could certainly face the uncertainty of ..."

Not even the greatest moralist ever, Jesus Himself, explained His parables. In fact, when His disciples asked, in essence, what in the world He was talking about, He often said, "He who has ears, let him hear." In other words, either you have spiritual insight, or you don't.

One of my favorite article purchases as magazine editor was a piece from a missionary wife. She told the story of her husband, a jungle doctor, not only ministering to a dying man's medical needs, but also sharing his faith with the man. All the while, she writes, she thought it was folly, that her husband was wasting his time with a man so incoherent and ill that he would never understand anyway.

In the end, she discovered that the man had heard and understood and even turned his life over to God. What I loved so much about the piece was that she managed to avoid the temptation to then make the larger point: that we should share our faith in the face of what may seem insurmountable obstacles. She simply told the story and stayed out of the way. I doubt one reader missed the point.

If you concentrate your efforts on the inspirational market, you will face this issue with nearly everything you write. An article—even for the general market—should never simply be *about* something; it must always be *for the purpose* of something. But never preach. Let the anecdotes make your point and assume the reader will get it.

A rule of thumb? The Golden Rule. Put yourself in the skin of your reader. Read your piece to yourself, and imagine how you would feel at the end of it. Does the story or nonfiction article make its own point? Has the writer (in this case, you) added a sermonette to the end? When in doubt, cut it out.

In the Left Behind series, fiction designed to communicate with both believers and the uninitiated, I had to walk a fine line between telling a story and preaching a sermon. My technique there was to introduce skeptical characters who had credibility and were not straw men.

Christianity is unique in that it is, in many ways, antireligious. Does that sound strange? Jesus said as much against religious leaders as He said on almost any other topic. His entire point was that salvation cannot be earned, but is a gift from God requiring true faith and belief.

Most Christians understand the difference between being religious (trying to follow a set of rules or perform good works in order to please God) and being a believer in Christ (trusting in Him for grace and forgiveness). But we must admit that, to the outsider, even that kind of talk seems religious. So get a skeptical character in there and have him say so: "'You talk about not being religious, and I'm telling you, you're the most religious person I know!'" I enjoy having Christian characters talk about the fact that they don't consider themselves religious, in the hearing of people who think they are nuts. As the characters argue, serious points can be made without the text feeling preachy.

So you see, dear reader ... Oops. Okay, I'm going to give you some credit for getting the point.

SETTING THE SCENE

Because of the proliferation of all sorts of visual media these days, it's more important than ever that we novelists write with the eye in mind. Fortunately, just as in the days of radio, what can be produced in the theater of the mind (in our case, the reader's mind) is infinitely more creative than what a filmmaker can put on the screen.

Be visual in your approach. People buy tickets to the movies or subscribe to cable channels hoping to see something they've never seen before. A good novel can provide the same, only—because of the theater of the mind—millions of readers can see your story a million different ways.

Although I'm encouraging you to be visual, I eschew too much description. I loved it when great potboiler writer John D. MacDonald described a character simply as "knuckly." A purist might have demanded hair length and color, eye size and shape and color, height, weight, build, gait. Not me. "Knuckly" gave me all I needed to picture the man. And if I saw him thinner, taller, older than you did, so much the better. MacDonald offered a suggestion that allowed his readers to populate their own scenes.

I recall an editor asking me to expand on my "oily geek" computer techie in one of the Left Behind volumes. I argued: (1) he was an orbital character, and while I didn't want him to be a cliché from central casting, neither did I feel the need to give him more characteristics than he deserved; and (2) he was there to serve a purpose, not to take over the scene, and certainly not to take over the book.

The editor countered, "But the reader will want to *see* him, and you haven't told us enough. Like, I see him in his twenties, plump, pale, with longish greasy hair and thick glasses."

What could I say? "Eureka! You just proved my point! All I wrote was that he was an oily geek, and look what you brought to the table."

Every reader has his own personal vision of a computer techie, so why not let each mental creation have its fifteen seconds of fame on the theater screen of the mind?

COINCIDENCES

In real life, I love coincidences. I'm fascinated by them. In fiction, more than one in each novel is too many, and even the one has to be handled well. (In comedies, sure, coincidences are fun and expected. How many times in *Seinfeld* do the characters run into the same people they tangled with earlier in the story?)

Say you invent a yarn about two people who marry, come to hate each other, and get divorced. Years pass, and each fails at yet another marriage. Available again, they run in to each other thousands of miles from home at a bazaar in Turkey. *Bizarre* is more like it. People won't buy it. If the couple reconnected at their high school reunion, that would be plausible, or if they both chickened out of that event at the same time and ran in to each other at a fast-food place nearby, that would be an interesting, more believable coincidence.

Q & A WITH JERRY

Is there any place for coarse language in inspirational fiction?

The short answer is no. The Christian Booksellers Association (CBA) market generally won't accept it. I might feel a characterization would be deeper and more realistic if I included gritty talk that wasn't gratuitous. But the sad fact is that it won't sell. If a CBA publisher wants to publish a manuscript with an expletive in it, a certain segment of its audience—primarily the gatekeepers (bookstore owners)—might refuse to market it, so publisher and author have to decide whether it's worth missing out on a whole segment of the market. For me, that's a no-brainer. I get around the problem by simply saying, "He swore," then quoting the rest of the character's sentence.

Is foreshadowing valid?

Oh, sure, but it can also be overused. I've long felt that I was clunky and intrusive in chapter one of *Left Behind* when I wrote that Rayford Steele was repulsed by his wife's new religious kick:

> Would it fade, her preoccupation with the end of the world, with the love of Jesus, with the salvation of souls? Lately she had been reading everything she could get her hands on about the Rapture of the church.

So, what happens next? The Rapture. I wince when I read that, but on the other hand, it's hard to argue with the success of that book. I'd like to think I've learned a thing or two in the decade since. If I had it to do over, I'd make that less overt. When foreshadowing, emphasize the *shadowing*. It should be just a glimpse, a hint.

What's the most common error you see in beginner's manuscripts?

Too many words. A man stands at the railing on a ferry crossing the harbor. His eyes dart, his breath is short, and he's running his hands through this hair. Next, the would-be novelist tells me the guy was tense, nervous, and worried. Thanks. I got that. Move straight to his thoughts: *"Will Julie be there when I get home?"*

Now I'm intrigued. Who's Julie, and why does she have him so agitated? The story is what has brought him to this point.

You've heard it before and will again: Don't tell me, show me. Some start by telling, then showing. They write, "Bill was nervous" and then show him being nervous. Give the reader credit. Skip the telling. The showing will tell.

Are transitions essential tools?

I'm from the school that says writers should rarely rely on transitional words and phrases. That will get me in trouble with classical writing teachers who love the *meanwhile*'s and the *by the same token*'s and the *on the other hand*'s. Some textbooks urge you to use a transitional word or phrase in the first sentence of every new paragraph. To my mind, these linking expressions will make your piece look like it was written for a class assignment.

If absolutely necessary, sure, use a transitional word or phrase. But skip it if you can. See how your writing flows without it. The right choice of words often negates the need.

Are flashbacks valid?

If used correctly, but they are fast falling out of favor. Many of the new fiction gurus recommend telling a story sequentially or using just one flashback. Maybe start near the present, flash back to the beginning, and use the entire manuscript to get back to square one. The last thing you want is a reader hitting a flashback that seems to explain everything, and thinking, *Well, why didn't you tell me?*

If you do feel the need for a flashback, make it clear, and be fair about it. I had to use a flashback in the first chapter of *Left Behind*, when Buck Williams, aboard Rayford's plane, recalls having been in Israel during an attack by Russia. I took the reader back with a clear setting change:

> A year and two months earlier, his January 1 cover story
> had taken him to Israel to interview Chaim Rosenzwieg
> and had resulted in the most bizarre event he had ever
> experienced.

After a few pages of recollections crucial to the plot, I brought
Buck and the reader back to the present:

> Buck remembered it vividly, as if it were yesterday. Had
> he not been there and seen it himself, he would not
> have believed it.

One problem with making the transition to a flashback is a tendency to remain in the past tense. Only in the first paragraph or two of the flashback do you need to employ past tense. Specifically, you should use the past perfect tense (*had* plus the past participle) at the beginning of the flashback, then switch to simple past tense for the remainder of the flashback. People realize what you're doing and where they are.

I like seamless flashbacks, so I make sure to shift gears only with the clutch engaged. In other words, I make sure that something in the present reminds the character why he is the way he is, and he tells that story as a flashback right within the present scene. Because you're in the character's head, the flashback can happen between lines of dialogue.

In one scene in *The Youngest Hero*, the character Miriam is narrating in the first person, telling the reader of an interaction with her son, when the subject of her former husband comes up. Saying none of this to her son, she simply recalls for the reader:

> He was always polite around girls, nodding, pretending
> to tip an imaginary hat whenever one walked by, which

was often in our big county high school. He gave off enough self-conscious shyness to take the edge off his swagger. We girls swooned.

Those are crucial details, part of the fabric of the story, but they work best as a flashback seamlessly woven into the present scene.

Is there a certain reading level you shoot for when writing for a mass audience?

Not consciously, but I was stunned to learn that *Reader's Digest* aims for an eighth-grade level. That sounded too young until I ran my own writing through a software program that told me my vocabulary was at a fifth-grade level. I feared that made my stuff sound too simple, but I realize it's that accessibility that can make books so popular. The critics may call it too simple, but I'm not writing for them.

What would be a quick list of writing do's?

Choose the simple word over the compound, and say what you mean. I believe in short paragraphs and tight dialogue. Every line written on normal, letter-size paper results in two lines of text in a magazine. If you write more than three lines in a paragraph, that's over an inch. Too many dense paragraphs, and people quit reading.

People like short paragraphs, pages with white space.

In books, variety in chapter size is also important. Two-page chapters and even single-paragraph chapters can work. Mega-bestselling author James Patterson has proved that.

If, in rereading your writing, you wonder whether a sentence works, stop wondering and fix it. I can assure you that if it made you hesitate, a large percentage of your audience won't get it and won't like it. If your own writing bores you in the least, your reader will slip into a coma. There's too much competition for you to settle for anything less than your best. Bestsellers start with the first word of the first line and hold you till the end. Write so your reader can't stand to put the book down.

Is there such a thing as a man's writer or a woman's writer?

Sure. Ring Lardner ("Shut up, he explained") is a man's writer. Zane Grey and Louis L'Amour were men's writers. Nicholas Sparks is a woman's writer. John Grisham is good for either gender. He can evoke emotion in male and female readers. I like to think I can write for both as well.

I once received a letter from a classmate I hadn't seen for decades. She had given up her faith, and was not a fan of the Left Behind series. I sent her *Though None Go With Me*, an overtly spiritual book with a female lead, and she liked it.

She told me she had never read a book by a man that so captured a woman's pain and perspective. That was particularly gratifying because I was one of four sons and have no sisters. But I was close to my mother and have always admired and respected women. Some would say I've gotten in touch with my feminine side.

One of my weird hobbies is to cover a byline with my thumb and try to guess the writer's gender just from the writing. I'm right more than half the time. Choice of words or manner of expression tips me off, though I'm often surprised and wrong.

Can a cliché ever work?

Clichés are clichés for good reason. They succinctly say something everybody knows. I use clichés in a first draft without thinking, then I go hunting for them, trying to change or eliminate them. If you come up with a fresh way to say something, good. But a well-worn cliché is better than a ridiculous new one. And often none is better than any.

What does it mean when writing seems to come too easily?

It means you run the risk of producing what Hollywood calls on-the-nose writing. That might sound positive, but it's not. It means you're writing things everyone already knows. Maybe they should call it on-the-*knows* writing. Beginning writers too often merely prove they know how life works. The best remedy is to start chopping.

Can a good writer break rules?

Yes, you can break rules—unless you do it because you're not thinking. If you're breaking a rule, do it on purpose.

Seasoned writers may be able to produce copy of a high quality faster than a less experienced person, but you should always strive to make your writing the best it can be.

If somebody wants a mere 400 words on a subject but can give me only ten minutes to write, I would hesitate to put my name on the piece. I'd want to spend an hour or two making it right.

Early in my career, I loved using one-word sentences. If I were writing in the first person, say, for a basketball coach, I would portray him as saying, "You may notice that I never use a whistle. Ever." Wow, what an added punch, eh?

A reviewer once wrote that I had "an irritating penchant for one-word sentences."

Guilty. Sorry.

ADVICE FOR THICK-SKINNED WRITERS

For all writing:

- **Maintain that thick skin.** Every piece of published writing is a duet between editor and writer, not a solo.

- **Omit needless words.**

- **Choose the normal word over the obtuse.**

- **Give the reader credit.** Avoid quotation marks around words used in another context, which imply that the reader wouldn't "get it" otherwise. (See how subtly insulting that is?)

- **Avoid being an adjectival maniac.** Good writing is a thing of strong nouns and verbs, not adjectives. Use adjectives sparingly. Novelist and editor Sol Stein says, "One plus one equals one-half," meaning the power of your words is diminished by not picking just the best one.

  Too much: His big, fluffy winter coat was warm and toasty.

  Better: He chose his toastiest coat and ventured out.

  Too much: The big, wet dog made its way down the hard, cold steps and nervously padded over to the red brick fireplace where he lay on a ratty, tattered carpet remnant.

Better: Buck shook the rain from his coat and gingerly made his way to the basement, where he stretched out on the piece of carpet before the fireplace.

- **Avoid throat-clearing.** Throat-clearing is an editor's term for a story or chapter that begins only after a page or two of scene-setting and background. Get on with it.
- **Avoid telling what's *not* happening.**

  He didn't respond.

  She didn't say anything.

  The crowded room never got quiet.

- **Avoid hedging your verbs**: "smiled *slightly*," "*almost* laughed," "frowned *a bit*," etc.
- **Avoid the term *literally* when you mean *figuratively*.**

  I ~~literally~~ died when I heard that.

  My eyes ~~literally~~ fell out of my head.

  I was ~~literally~~ climbing the walls.

- **You can often delete the word *that*.**
- **Avoid subtle redundancies.** "She nodded her head in agreement" contains a hat trick, a triple redundancy. The last four words could be deleted.

  He clapped ~~his hands~~. (What else would he clap?)

  She shrugged ~~her shoulders~~.

  He blinked ~~his eyes~~.

  They heard ~~the sound of~~ a train whistle.

- **Avoid incorrect use of the word *echo*:** "Her voice echoed in the empty house." Really? Unless the house was devoid of furniture, a voice wouldn't actually echo.

- **Avoid the words *up* and *down* unless they're really needed.**

   He rigged ~~up~~ the device.

   She sat ~~down~~ on the couch.

Especially in fiction (but also in nonfiction anecdotes):

- **Maintain a single point of view (POV) for every scene.** Switching POV within a scene is one of the most common errors beginning writers make.

- **Avoid clichéd scenes and situations, not just clichéd words and phrases.** Don't begin with the main character waking to an alarm clock; don't allow your character to describe herself while looking in a mirror; don't make future love interests literally bump into each other at first meeting.

- **Avoid on-the-nose writing** (writing that exactly mirrors real life without adding to the story).

- **Resist the urge to explain.**

   Marian ~~was mad. She~~ pounded the table. "George, you're going to drive me crazy," she said~~, angrily~~.

- **Show, don't tell.** If Marian pounds the table and chooses those words, we don't need to be told she's mad.

- **Avoid mannerisms in attributions.** People *say* things; they don't wheeze, gasp, sigh, laugh, grunt, snort, reply, retort, exclaim, or declare them.

   Not: John was exhausted. He dropped onto the couch and exclaimed tiredly, "I'm beat."

   Better: John dropped onto the couch. "I'm beat."

   Not: "I hate you," Jill hissed ferociously.

Better: "I hate you," Jill said, narrowing her eyes.

Sometimes people whisper or shout or mumble, but let your choice of words in the dialogue imply that they are doing so. If it's important that they sigh or laugh, separate the action from the dialogue: "Jim sighed. 'I just can't take any more,' he said." Usually you can even drop the attribution *he said* if you have described his action first, as in this example. We know who's speaking.

- **Specifics add the ring of truth.**

    The 4:06 train was two minutes late, Marge realized as she stood drying dishes before the window that looked out on the Burlington-Northern tracks to the west. She wondered if there had been a problem at the depot at Main and Walnut that would keep Jim from getting home on time.

- **Avoid similar character names.** In fact, avoid even the same first initials.

- **Avoid mannerisms of punctuation, type styles, and sizes.** "He ... was ... _DEAD_!" isn't any more dramatic than "He was dead." And the character is just as dead either way.

CHAPTER 13

Pursuing Publication

I know writers who collect rejection slips, hoard them, even paper their walls with them—specifically their bathrooms. Some writing coaches even urge their charges to try to rack up as many rejections as they can. I know they think that getting rejections proves writers are busy, in the game, producing work.

But *going* for rejections? That seems masochistic, and I have a better tack: I avoid rejection slips like radioactive waste. I don't want even one. Here's a revelation for you: I think they can be eliminated. You don't ever need to read another.

Here's how: Do your homework. Know what your target market is looking for. Sure, occasionally you'll hear back from a magazine or book publisher that your idea didn't ring a bell. But that's not a rejection. That's a business transaction. You did a bit of work, solicited their interest, they passed. You move on.

Now, if you had written the entire article or even whole book be-fore determining even an inkling of interest on the part of the editor, you probably deserved a rejection letter. Even if you're brand new to the writing game, save yourself mountains of fruitless work by trying to get an editor on board with you early. If you're new, she'll likely express only speculative interest (e.g., "Yes, it sounds interesting, and we'll be happy to give it a look, provided you ..."). It's what comes after that *provided you* that becomes your marching orders. Does she want it longer than you proposed? Shorter? In first person rather than third? Does she have suggestions for other angles, other people to interview?

To the best of your ability, do everything she suggests. You have a green light on spec, which is nearly as rare as a sale. And while she can still reject your submission, by proving yourself able to work with an editor, you're nearly forcing the editor to stick with you—even if your writing is light-years away from where it should be some day. She may ask for rewrites, bring a seasoned writer alongside, or assign you one of her best copyeditors. But by showing her that you have a thick skin, that you can take input, and that you recognize that a piece of published work is not a solo, but rather a duet between writer and editor, you've given yourself the best chance at a sale. And you've avoided rejection.

Veterans will tell you not to take rejections personally. That's a laugh, eh? If you're like me, your very soul is on that page. Let's be honest. The reason we want to avoid rejection letters is that no one wants to be rejected.

Our goal as writers should be to write better than we, our spouses, our parents, or our editors dreamed possible. That's my wish for you, and that's why I'm trying to stuff this book with practical tips and proven strategy. Now that you're ready to dive in, let's debunk a few myths. I'll be blunt and let you in on a few things I wish I'd learned early in my career.

Writing is hard work. Don't agree so quickly. Wait till you've been dragged across the bumpy road toward publication a few times. For now, admit that you suspect you're something special. The exceptional exception. For you, writing will be a breeze. Editors will clamor for your work. You foresee a bidding war over your next book, with your bank account the big winner. Is that *Reader's Digest* on the phone?

Not so fast.

I was talking with an editor friend the other day, a veteran of many writers conferences, who has seen all levels of competency. "It's rare that you find a first-timer who really gets it," she said. What first-timers don't get is that writing is not a hobby, a spare-time activity, or something to play at. It's work.

It's a calling, like it or not.

For me, writing is as exhausting as physical labor. After writing (and publishing) more than 150 books, that still surprises me. Sometimes, on deadline, I'll sit at the keyboard for six, eight, ten hours or more. When I'm finished, I'm as spent as if I've been ditch-digging all day. I don't understand it. It doesn't seem that physically taxing, but it is. I guess it's the fact that you must be constantly thinking in order to write.

Creativity will cost you, wear you out. Don't ever get the idea writing is easy. If it is, you're not working hard enough. I can't tell you the number of writers who agree that the stuff that comes easy takes the most rewriting. And the stuff that comes hard reads the easiest.

Writing takes specialized skills. A psychologist friend once asked if I would have lunch with him and give him a few tips. "I'm thinking about doing a little freelance writing in my spare time," he said.

"Really," I said. "That's interesting, because I've been thinking about doing a little psychological counseling in my spare time."

"I didn't know you were trained for that."

"Gotcha," I said.

When you hang out your shingle as a writer, be prepared for un-intended slights like that. People tell me all the time that they have a book in them, if they only had the time to write. That would be like my saying I have a sermon in me, if only I had the time to prepare it. Pulpit work is a calling, a discipline, something a person is trained and set apart for. Writing is rarely accorded the same respect as other professions, but if people want to tell themselves they could be the

About Editors

For years I was a magazine publisher and editor, and for more years I was a book publisher. Knowing from experi-ence what I faced from people like me—the gatekeepers for magazines and books—I developed a realistic approach to my own freelancing. I knew what editors really thought of poor, sloppy work. Our letters and notes to would-be writ-ers were kind and cordial, but having been on the editori-al side of the desk, I knew the freelance writer reputation I wanted to avoid.

Sorry to break this to you, but behind closed doors, edi-tors say things you wouldn't want to hear. To cut the ten-sion, we editors would put our occasionally scathing com-ments on evaluation sheets meant for our colleagues' eyes only. We could be beautifully, brutally honest.

One editor friend, instead of commenting on a manuscript that had made the rounds, taped a match to the evaluation sheet.

Another manuscript arrived with a postcard saying that we had better hurry with our decision, because the author had other irons in the fire. An editor suggested, "Let's urge her to remove one of the irons and make room for the manuscript."

That may make you wonder if editors exist only to make your life miserable. While they would never—except in the case of a most embarrassing accident—actually mail a note like the ones I mentioned, editors are the source of generic rejection letters that crush hope. And some editors do suffer from terminal indigestion. As long as we're being honest, yes, there are even those editors who feel glee at weak writing because it somehow affirms the injustice of their own writing not having found purchase.

But most editors remain hopeful they'll find something worthwhile in their stacks of submissions. They're looking for a writer with that something special. They want you to succeed.

Often, we editors would get letters from people saying that they'd graduated from this or that school with a certain degree and were now ready for an assignment. But we weren't looking for writers who were simply available. We were looking for writers with ideas and the other *-ilities*: adaptability, coachability, flexibility.

> It bears repeating that an editor may ask many things of you and make several suggestions. If you follow those directives to the letter, even if your writing is subpar for now, the editor will want to work with you. This puts her on your side.

one-in-a-thousand writer who could sell a manuscript to a book publisher, if they could only find the time, fine.

It's not you against the world. Don't think of writing as competitive. This is tough. Nearly impossible. We all compare ourselves to our peers, worrying who's winning, who's publishing more, selling more, earning more, enjoying more visibility. You might think, *That's easy for you to say, now that you've arrived.* Maybe. But anyone who has succeeded was once an unknown beginner. I decided a long time ago that I could only be the best writer I could be. I had to stop worrying about where my writing put me in the pecking order. I have no control over the success of a project in the marketplace. And if my book sells a hundred times more than another writer's, that doesn't make me a better writer.

My goals are internal. If I succeed in being the best I can be—maximizing my potential, taking no shortcuts—and this success makes me the thousandth best writer in my field, am I not ahead of the writer who is number one and yet still not doing his best work? Stop comparing. The world is full of wonderful writers. There are apprentices, journeymen, craftsmen, and bestselling authors. Sometimes the bestselling author is a master craftsman, sometimes not. What matters is where you are on your journey, striving to be the best you can be.

I need to grow and learn. I read everything I can find on the craft of writing. My goal is to write better this week than last, this year than last. Where that places me on the spectrum of writers is irrelevant. Who but me would care, anyway? That's all about ego, and worrying about it won't make me a better writer.

A little secret: Once you've come to grips with the comparison gremlins, you can actually be happy for another writer who succeeds (rejoice with those who rejoice) and quit entertaining the green-eyed monster.

Even "sacred" writing can be edited. The words you choose, regardless of how completely you have surrendered yourself and your work to God, are not sacred. Only Scripture is God-breathed. However, the *result* of your writing might very well be sacred. I split hairs for a reason. *Sacred* can mean "untouchable," and it can mean "godly." If you regard your writing as sacred in the sense of "untouchable" (*God gave me these words, so don't edit them*), they had better be divinely perfect, or God gets a bad rap. Frankly, writers who make this claim—and it happens often—are immediately branded as amateurs. An inside joke among editors in inspirational publishing is that God is the worst literary agent ever.

If you really believe your writing is beyond reproach, beyond question, beyond improvement, then you've made it an idol or you're deluding yourself. We've all been there. It hurts to give an editor free rein to cut and shred the work we'd prefer to believe was dictated by God Himself. Are we giving the editor a break, or protecting ourselves from criticism, when we inform her that God has already ordained every word?

Doing your best writing is only step one. I never think of submitting a piece of writing that I think I can still improve upon. The emphasis there is on *I*. I'm not saying *no one* can make it better. Fresh eyes are always valuable, but avoid the temptation to tell an editor, "I'm sure this needs more work, but here it is." Submit the absolute best work you can do, and then be open to input. It's a duet, remember, not a solo.

Editors are sometimes wrong. At the risk of seeming contradictory, I must also advise that you not automatically agree with every suggestion your editor makes. (Of course, your confidence—and freedom—in this area will, and should, grow with your publishing experience.) Any humble editor would agree that editing is largely subjective. Often, an editor has a better idea of what works than you do. And editors should better understand their readers.

They're usually right, but not always. Sometimes you must plead your case. To avoid being labeled belligerent, choose your fights carefully. Speak your mind kindly. Your editor, I hope, will do the same.

It's okay to ask an editor to explain herself. But ultimately, you need to submit both your words and your will. Unless you're publishing a book yourself (which I rarely recommend), someone else is assigned to make the call.

The editor exists to satisfy readers. Putting the reader first may mean putting you, the writer, second. That's the way it is. Live with it and learn to put your priorities on the same plane as the editor's.

Learn *The Elements of Style*. While I espouse wide reading in the area of writing, few single books can make an immediate, significant improvement in a writer like Strunk and White's *The Elements of Style*. It's a small volume worth reading annually, and it contains advice on everything from clear writing to punctuation to avoiding needless words. I've never seen so much information packed into one thin book.

Ignore writer's block. I quarrel with anyone claiming she can't write because of writer's block. The answer to writer's block is Nike's motto: Just do it.

We all get stuck, but that's when the fun and creative flow we enjoyed yesterday becomes a job today. We still have to sit there and do our work. As I've said, if I were a factory worker or an executive, I wouldn't be able to call in and plead worker's block. Imagine what I'd hear from my boss. Some days, you won't have the inspiration, and your muse will be on strike. But if you don't write today, you're going to pay for it tomorrow. As your own boss, you can allow yourself the freedom to take a day off, as long as you understand the consequences.

Ernest Hemingway allotted himself a certain number of hours to work, and when the time came for him to break, he would stop in mid-sentence. That made it a punishment to stop and a reward to get back to work. When he returned to the manuscript, he knew exactly where he was.

Old rules still apply in the digital age. The Internet and e-mail make life easier for everybody. I'm old enough to remember buying manuscript boxes and packing up my precious babies to ship to publishers. Today, I attach my manuscripts to e-mails and transmit them in seconds.

But be sure to use the same level of professionalism when sending electronic documents as you did when using snail mail. I'm appalled at how sloppy people are on the Internet and in e-mail. Punctuation and spelling go out the window, and it often appears that people are making words up as they go along. Just for the sake of discipline and reputation, I try to make sure that anything I write, even a brief note— and boy, can they be brief—is spelled and punctuated correctly.

In many cases, especially when you're communicating with editors and publishers, your prospects for publication may depend on how you come across via the Internet. Leave nothing to chance.

Quality and timing trump quantity. Don't annoy your editor. It's okay to send an occasional e-mail to let her know you're available, but it's even better to query her on a great idea. Much more than that is unprofessional and presumes upon her time.

Many Web sites are hungry for content. Competition is fierce, and the pay is often poor. But with so many online sources—many tied to print publications—any writer should be able to find a place to publish. Research to find sites that match your interests, and then submit story ideas.

Once you've scored with such a Web site, print those articles and use them as clips with prospective magazine or newspaper editors.

Read about the craft. Subscribe to a writer's magazine. Read books on writing. If your goal is the inspirational market, at least two volumes are no-brainers for your library: Sally E. Stuart's *Christian Writers' Market Guide* and *The Christian Writer's Manual of Style.*

If you're into religious writing that is not specifically Christian, search for publishing guides in your discipline. There are enough differences in guidelines within Christian publishing alone that it should be no surprise that other faiths have their different emphases and approaches. A big mistake inspirational writers make is to assume that anything spiritual is fair game for any religious publisher. If you've been a person of faith for any length of time, you know that each denomination and publication and publishing house has its own list of preferences and taboos. Disregarding or not knowing these is the quickest path to a returned manuscript.

Be careful what you wish for. An assignment I should have turned down was a resource for teenagers called *Light on the Heavy*, in essence, Bible doctrine made easy. The assumption was that I understood enough of doctrine to explain it to someone else. I know the basics, but I'm neither theologian nor scholar, and writing that book was

About Deadlines

One thing I learned by being on the other side of the desk for so many years is how few people understand what a deadline is, especially in the book business. When I was vice president for publishing at Moody Bible Institute and in charge of Moody Press, I discovered that only about 1 percent of our writers made their deadlines. Some were within a day or two; others, within a week or two. Most were within a month or two. Some, within a year or two. But actually having the manuscript in our hands by the date on the contract? It only happened with about one in a hundred authors.

I had long been pretty good about deadlines, although in the book business they clearly weren't set in stone. No one was tossing my pages or my set type into a boiling cauldron when I was late. But learning that merely achieving my deadline would put me in the top 1 percent of contracted authors changed my attitude. My deadlines have become sacrosanct. I can't tell you the number of publishers who have said, "Wow, you actually made your deadline." It may not seem like a big deal, but when the odds against having a book published are a thousand to one, separating yourself from 99 percent of the competition *is* a big deal.

I tried to teach my kids that if they simply do their jobs, they'll stand out like sore thumbs. And people who come to work on time or even a bit early make an even better impression. Get your research and writing done, turn your projects in early, and you'll shine.

sheer torture. I learned a lot in the process, but it was an awful season of writing. I'm gratified that it succeeded at a certain level. I even heard from the occasional seminarian who said he used it as a primer. But I learned what kind of a project to turn down, even at a stage of my career when I hardly ever said no.

Look for new vistas. Take no short-cuts and expect many detours. My first eighteen books were all nonfiction, and were my ideas from start to finish. I had to find people I thought were worthy of biographies, then talk publishers into the projects. Once I had a little success in sports autobiographies, publishers would occasionally ask if I was available to write another book. Eventually, as far as personality books went, about half were the publishers' ideas and half mine.

I got my start in fiction through a casual conversation with a former boss, Stanley C. Baldwin. He was freelance editing a set of novels, and mentioned that the publisher was looking for another title. Did I want a shot at it?

Not all nonfiction writers can write fiction, but I had an idea and gave it a try. That novel, *Margo*, became a thirteen-book series. The first appeared in the late 1970s, and I still get letters about it today.

One of the most encouraging seasons of my life came when I met Roy Carlisle, then an editor at Harper & Row, at a writers conference in California. I was there as an editor and speaker, and naturally he had never heard of me. He was amused by some of my humor and asked what I was writing. I was in the middle of the *Margo* series, and so I showed him the first few volumes. He read one while at the conference.

I told him one of my lifelong dreams was to write a novel for a major publisher, and one publisher that had always piqued my interest was Harper & Row. Roy was blunt but encouraging. He said my fiction showed promise, but that I wasn't ready for the big time yet. Not exactly what I wanted to hear. Roy's counsel was to keep writing my mystery series and to keep sending them to him. He'd know when I was ready.

My first standalone international thriller, *The Operative*, was published by Harper & Row in 1987.

Experience is its own reward. What do I know now that I wish I'd known when I first started writing? How interested people would be in End Times prophecy.

As for what I'm glad I didn't know? The odds against ever getting published. On the other hand, if telling you those odds scares you off, maybe you *should* be scared off. I assume you're still reading because you want to be the one to beat the odds. And the way to do that is to learn every trick of the trade, every mistake made by those who preceded you, and every tip that will give you a leg up.

One advantage of being a working journalist before I tried freelancing was the opportunity to network. I also got to see the mistakes that freelancers made before I was in a position to make them. They came across my desk every day, so I knew what to avoid.

Success breeds success. The better you do, the better known your work becomes, and the easier it is to sell more. As I've said, editors are looking for the next worthy author. Strive to be their next discovery, the find every editor is hoping for. While you're still learning, still honing your craft, deliver clean copy on time. This may result in another assignment. Prove yourself easy to work with.

Check out the competition. Writers read. Check out the stuff at the top of the charts. Even edgy stuff. Sure, if it's clear something is too raw for your sensibilities, feel free to pass. But you'd be surprised what you can learn by those at the top of their game. Find writers trying something new, and decide for yourself whether it works. Incorporate a style or approach only if it seems to work with your unique voice.

You can learn from those kinds of examples, just as you can learn from other freelancers who have learned how to be superproductive. A woman who used to work for me is now a freelancer with thirty to forty articles and two or three book ideas circulating all the time; she has them catalogued and is constantly writing, researching, mailing, or proofreading. For her, writing is a job and a business. She knows that the more proposals and queries she creates, the better chance she has at selling and being published. One thing she doesn't do is collect rejection slips.

ABOUT PITCHING

When pitching ideas to editors, don't feel compelled to tell them what you haven't done. There's no need to say you're brand new at this, that you have never written, let alone been published. Just identify yourself as a freelance writer and make your proposal. If you have no clips to show or experience to list, the editor will get the picture.

And by all means, avoid the telltale signs of an amateur: quills in your logo, or typewriters, or the words *writer, speaker, author,* etc. Let your classy, understated, readable stationery speak for itself. The more you've done, the less you have to say.

When I had written four books, I listed them all. When I had written several dozen, I mentioned that and listed a recent title or two. Now I might mention Left Behind, in case they're wondering if I'm *that* Jenkins.

If you're new, "I'm a freelance writer and here's my plan," works best. Give the gist of your article idea and put it in the context of the magazine. "Reading your recent piece on the American market for domestic cheeses made me think you might be interested in an article on the Eastern Seaboard's most prolific purveyors of ..."

I successfully pitched *Hemispheres*, the magazine of United Airlines, on using a piece out of my book *As You Leave Home* by mentioning that many fellow flyers were my age and undoubtedly also lamenting their teenagers going off to college, the military, or the work force.

Once, while editor of *Moody* magazine, I received an excellent article on how to wash your dog. Problem was, it could have been a Pulitzer Prize winner, but it didn't fit our publication. If it had been "How to Wash Your Dog Without Getting Your Bible Wet," we might have bitten. Too few writers do their homework. Pitch articles that make sense based on your research on a specific magazine. Otherwise, you're wasting everyone's time, especially your own.

Here are my top tips for query letters and proposals.

1. Never write to *Dear Sir* or *To Whom It May Concern*. Take the time to find out whom you're corresponding with and write directly to the appropriate person.

2. Do not use colored paper as stationery. Editors seem to universally see this as a sign of an amateur.

3. Do not use bold or larger-than-normal type anywhere in a letter or manuscript, and never use more than one font.

4. Your title must be positive, not negative. Not: "How Depression Can Defeat You," but rather: "Winning Over Depression."

5. A manuscript must have type on only one side of each page and must be double-spaced (not single- or triple-spaced, or spaced at the 1.5 setting on your word processor).

6. A manuscript should never be bound, stapled, clipped, or in a notebook. Editors want the pages in a stack, loose, with each page numbered and carrying the author's name.

7. The word *by* rarely appears on the cover of a book unless it is self-published, and even then it is the sign of an amateur.

8. The misspelling of the word *acknowledgments* (as *acknowledgements*, a British variation) or *foreword* (as *forward*) is another clue that you're an amateur. *Foreword* means "before the text"; it consists of *fore* and *word*, and has nothing to do with direction.

9. Your manuscript should not have justified right margins. Use ragged right margins, the kind that makes your manuscript appear to have been typed rather than computer generated. Justified margins cause inconsistent spacing between words, which make for difficult reading for overworked editors.

10. A common cliché in inspirational books is to include prayers in prefatory material. Even paraphrasing those to say, "My prayer is that God would ..." is better than, "Lord, I pray ...", but avoid either in the dedication or acknowledgments ("Lord, thank you for my wonderful editor ..." *Blech!*).

11. You've heard the slogan *just do it*. Now, learn to just say it. Imagine yourself telling your story to a friend or writing a letter. Good writing is not about loads of adjectives and adverbs. It consists of powerful nouns and verbs. So many beginners fall into an overwrought style I call "writtenese." Your relatives may love your flowery language, and perhaps your unpublished creative writing teacher does too, but read what sells. Usually you'll find it simple and straightforward.

Take note. Your goal as a beginner is to set yourself apart from the thousand other writers trying to score with your publisher at the same time. Make the adjustments recommended in these pages for a better chance at acceptance. Publishers get so much material (many publishing only one-tenth of a percent of what they receive) that any of the above mistakes gives first readers a reason to pass on your piece.

ABOUT SELF-PUBLISHING

Excepting rare circumstances when a professional must publish or perish, I am not one who advocates self-publishing. Clearly, certain types of work, such as family histories or small works that aren't intended for a larger audience, should be self-published. But writers should write for publication; they should study and learn and grow with the selling of their work in mind. Don't pay to have something published unless it is not intended for the masses. Let publishers pay you because you have become a writer people want to read.

That goes against the grain of popular thought, I know. There seems to be some glamour in bypassing the system, telling New York that they can ignore you for only so long, and asking what do they know, anyway. But there is no glamour in a garage full of unsold self-published books. Yes, there are self-published successes, and when these hit, they are often recognized by legitimate publishers and become real books. *Writer's Digest* fields an annual contest to recognize self-published books that somehow missed the notice of conventional publishers. But the ultimate prize of the competition is being picked up by a major house and gaining real credibility by having the book released to the broader book trade.

There is nothing like the imprimatur of a traditional publishing house's logo on the spine of your book.

Q & A WITH JERRY

What do you think of critique groups?

Sorry, I'm a maverick in this area, even disagreeing with many of my most trusted and admired and respected colleagues, who swear by critique groups. My biggest fear is that they too often result in the blind leading the blind. Someone (published or not) with a strong personality could say something about your writing and crush you, right or wrong. And too often, such groups can deteriorate into gripe and whine sessions, with much of the group's time spent complaining about lesser writers who somehow sell, publishers who don't care about quality, and all the rest.

If you can find a writing critique group run by an upbeat, encouraging (but honest), experienced author or editor, then sure, go for it. If it proves helpful, and you find yourself growing and succeeding, stay with it. Otherwise, let the marketplace critique you.

How do you feel about writers conferences?

I'm definitely for them, and have been to dozens of good ones over the years. My own Christian Writers Guild hosts an annual event at the Broadmoor Hotel in Colorado Springs. But such gatherings must not take the place of your regular, steady writing efforts. A writers conference should serve as a fueling station. Come and get filled with inspiration, and then get back to your desk.

People who attend writers conferences and never get around to writing are like the wannabes who find the writing life attractive but never sell anything. They may even wear what they consider writer's clothes: Hush Puppies and corduroys and sweaters with patches on the elbows. They might even smoke a pipe. But they go to the same writers conferences year after year, rubbing shoulders with freelancers, editors, publishers, and agents, and rarely leave with anything to show for it.

As I've said, there's only one way to write, and that is with seat in chair.

At the best writers conferences, expect to stay up late talking and brainstorming and networking. Soak up everything, consider new ideas and approaches. Go home exhausted. The first week home should be busy. Write the editors. Send the proposal you pitched and revised. Use the conference as a jumping-off place, but not as an end in itself.

Is an agent required in today's market?

It's getting that way, but you may find securing an agent as hard as landing a publisher. Most publishers now prefer working with agents, because doing so protects both sides. If you have an agent, you're not likely to accuse a publisher of trying to take advantage of you.

Naturally, while many agents are looking for the next great writer and may give beginners a look, most need a stable of producing freelancers who can make them some money. Early in your career, send proposals to publishers that accept unsolicited manuscripts (some still do). Once you get an offer, rest assured you'll find an agent interested in representing you. Obviously, agents love having a commodity in which someone has already shown interest.

Agents work for their percentage; if you don't make money, neither do they. Your agent will push to get your work in print.

AFTERWORD

Keeping the Goal in Sight

Living in the aftermath of 9/11 has changed how Americans view the world. We no longer have the option of avoiding the traumatic in favor of the familiar.

I was writing about the apocalypse, so naturally, such horror informed my work, as it should any contemporary writer's.

On that fateful day in 2001, I was about thirty blocks north of the World Trade Center, at breakfast with a publisher to promote a new book. We had just taped an interview with Bryant Gumbel for the CBS *Early Show*, scheduled to air September 24. Needless to say, it never made it to the screen.

It took us twenty-four hours to find a rental car and leave Manhattan via the George Washington Bridge. Behind us, the towers had been replaced by billowing smoke. The assault on every sense will stick with me forever, along with the grief and the horrible realization of how vulnerable we are. For my whole life I had been insulated against such mayhem by decades and oceans. No more.

Months later we visited Ground Zero, a hole too big to comprehend until it was brought into perspective by the sight of a cement truck at the bottom that looked like a toy.

I was struck that our job as writers is to provide that kind of perspective, touch points to make clear the enormity of the themes we examine. Though we may be writing fiction, if our focus is clear, we reveal reality in all its pain and joy. And as inspirational writers, we have a duty to do justice to a worldview that may bend but will never be crushed under the weight of hopelessness.

There is a place for the stark reality of the kind of writing that despairs of the seeming hopelessness of man's inhumanity to man. And while we must not flinch in the face of such a bleak worldview, our burden, our task, our privilege is to represent hope. That doesn't mean Pollyanna stories in which everyone lives happily ever after—at least this side of heaven. People still suffer. Innocents still die. But we are believers, and if we cannot crack the door to hope, we dare not call ourselves inspirational writers.

GETTING OUT OF THE WAY

The toughest challenge for any artist, any creator, is to resist the urge to show off. Our name will be on the cover, after all, and we'd love to remind the reader with a turn of phrase or a choice word that yes, it's me fashioning this message.

But the best writers, like the best composers and painters, know that it is not about them. It is about the art, the content—and anything that interferes with the connection between that and the viewer, listener, or reader is an interruption.

If your reader is aware of your technique, he may miss your message. If the pianist dazzles his audience with technique, the purpose of the composer may be compromised. If the appreciator of art becomes aware of the brushstrokes, the artist may lose his ability to reach the soul through the meat of his message.

A true classic transports you. You're unaware of the performance and the performer, the author and his technique. As creators, that should be our goal. Not to write classics. That's not up to us. The market will decide that. But to get out of the way so the heart of the message reaches the soul of the reader.

Accomplish this by writing clearly and concisely, enticing your readers and guiding them to the core of your work. Use words they will understand rather than ones that will make them wonder. Get out of the way of your art.

THE DESTINATION

I like movies that are not afraid to be quiet. The film adaptation of John Irving's *The Cider House Rules* is a masterpiece, which I confess despite the fact that my philosophy is diametrically opposed to its message. Irving deserved his Academy Award, and I applauded his acceptance speech, wherein he made clear his worldview. He didn't pretend he didn't have a message.

And neither should we. Ours is a message of hope, of reconciliation, of forgiveness. True art will communicate that without preaching. Give the reader credit. Tell a story and assume he gets it.

If the Left Behind books, *The Prayer of Jabez*, *The Purpose-Driven Life*, *Your Best Life Now*, and others have awakened the general market to the vast potential of inspirational titles, the horizon has been broadened for us all.

Now is the time for honest, perhaps painful, self-assessment. If you have what it takes, including skin thick enough to endure the honest evaluation of your work, you can succeed in making the most of every opportunity.

I'm living my dream as a full-time freelance novelist, writing about things I believe in and care about. And you can too. The path is crowded and the passage long, but the reward is worth it. You can write for the benefit of your soul. And you can write to reach the soul of another.

Welcome to the journey.

HITTING HOME

The summer of 1965 broke hot and humid in northern Illinois. And when a six-foot, 200-and-something-pound 15-year-old nicknamed Moose showed up at Camp Hickory for a term as a junior counselor to 9- and 10-year-olds, he was ready for some fun.

Moose was from the suburbs, a baseball player just off a championship season. As one of four sons, he expected to identify with his young charges and teach them a thing or two about sports—maybe even about God. The Baptist General Conference camp in Round Lake, Illinois, was all wood cabins and meeting houses with slapping screen doors, but there were also volleyball and badminton nets, a ball diamond, horseshoe pits, tetherball poles, hiking trails, and a pool.

Air conditioning didn't exist at Camp Hickory. After an afternoon of sweating through his clothes in the sun, Moose and other staff cohorts would sneak into the walk-in cooler behind the dining hall. The blast of frigid air was nearly intoxicating, making the re-emergence to humid reality shocking.

Moose served under an elderly counselor named Joe Pierce, who had been part of a rival gang to Al Capone in the 1930s before coming to Christ. Old Joe and his stories made an idyllic week all the more magical. Days and nights were spent at dining hall meals, the flagpole, handicraft sessions, sports, evening meetings, devotions, and bedtime chats. Moose regaled his junior boys with stories of the Rapture and what might happen if it occurred during rush hour.

Moose was one of those teenagers who had never been in trouble. Raise in a devout Christian home, he had become a believer as a young child, and he enjoyed everything about Sunday school and church. Looking forward to his junior year in a sprawling public high school, Moose was laid back about his faith. He didn't want to push his beliefs on anyone.

But at Camp Hickory, leading a camper to Christ was a thrill. No one looked at you sideways if you read Scripture aloud or led in prayer.

THE BIG GAME

The highlight of the week arrived. A local church softball team, Cumberland Baptist, was coming to play the staff. Moose knew this team. His own Elk Grove Baptist Church team had played them and lost soundly. They were led by a superstar player named Johnny Ankerberg, a collegian who was also a young preacher and nephew of Camp Directors Dan and Joyce Ankerberg. He was a friend of Moose's friends, and Moose was proud to know him.

That afternoon, the young staff had one of those games. They upset the experienced, much better Cumberland team, with Moose scoring the winning run in the bottom of the last inning. But better than that, Johnny Ankerberg himself congratulated Moose and asked—in front of people—what he should speak on that night in the service.

He's asking me? Moose thought. *Well, of course. I've been here all week, I ought to know.*

Moose had heard Ankerberg speak before and knew he was powerful and incisive. "Well," he said, "there are a lot of phonies here. Maybe something on really being what you say you are all the time."

SOUL STIRRING

Everyone got cleaned up, enjoyed a noisy dinner in the mess hall, and then settled in for the evening service. There were skits and music, and finally it was time for John Ankerberg to speak. Moose sat with old Joe Pierce and their boys, waiting to counsel any who wanted to receive Christ or rededicate their lives.

Ankerberg jumped right into his topic, goading, challenging, questioning the crowd: "Are you really a Christian, or are you just playing at it? Do you paste a smile on your face and sit still in church but sneak around doing bad things with your friends at school and on the weekends?"

Not me, Moose thought. *I know better. No smoking or drinking or vandalism. I don't even swear.*

Moose noticed that other staff seemed self-conscious. Some of the campers squirmed. *Good. Johnny's getting to 'em, just like I hoped.*

But then Ankerberg shifted gears. "Maybe you're not doing anything wrong," he suggested. "Maybe you think you're okay with the Lord."

Right, Moose thought. Now you're talking. Preach it, John.

Suddenly, it seemed as if there were no others in the room but Moose and John. As the big teenager sat staring at the preacher, John began to hit home. "Do your friends even know you're a believer? Or are you a secret-service Christian, saving your piety for Sundays and home? Will your friends risk hell because you've never even told them about Jesus?

Moose's pulse raced. Was he one of the phonies he himself had referred to? This was getting way too personal. John began a litany of the dangers of keeping quiet about your faith; how the world and friends and influences could rob you of your first love of Christ. How people you care about could be lost forever because you were afraid of offending them. *How does he know?*

"Who will stem the tide of invisible Christians?" John thundered, and suddenly Moose knew personally what the old term meant, falling under conviction. He shuddered, his heart galloping. "After what Jesus did for you on the cross, can you not suffer a little embarrassment for Him. I'm looking for young people who will say, 'I will stand for Christ by God's grace, even if I have to stand alone!'"

How Moose wanted to take that stand! If God would give him the courage and power, he could do it!

THE CHANGE

John finally asked for people to stand if they were ready to make that commitment, and Moose leapt to his feet. He was near tears, ready to burst.

"A counselor is already standing," John said, "ready to pray with you about this."

Oh, no! How could Moose counsel anyone while under conviction himself, eager to get right with God, desperate to seek forgiveness for having been a secret Christian?

But a nine-year-old boy was delivered to him. Moose talked with him, prayed with him, and then found everyone else occupied. He could hold it in no longer. He ran from the screened-in assembly hall, out into the darkness past the fellowship hall, and into the parking lot, where he found a friend's car. It was unlocked. He jumped in and lay across the front seat, sobbing and crying out to God for forgiveness.

"I *will* share my faith! I *will* tell others about You! I don't care what they think about me or even if they ever agree. I want to be the kind of believer You want me to be."

When Moose finally left that car, he sensed God's forgiveness and even felt his first infusion of courage. He sought out friends and told them boldly of his new resolve.

The rest of the week was different, at least inwardly. There was still the fun and the sports and the sweat and the cooler. But the meetings and the private times with campers took on a new urgency and import. This would not be one of those annual re-dedications that didn't "take." Moose felt like a new person.

BACK TO SCHOOL

At the end of the summer, just before school began, Moose talk-ed to John Ankerberg into coming into his home to share the same message with his youth group and guests. Moose's older brother Jeff had the same response, and when they went back to Forest View High School as a junior and a senior, things had changed.

Moose carried his Bible atop his books, feeling conspicuous and, frankly, scared. But the conversations sparked by friends' questions resulted in several of them becoming believers. His and Jeff's new commitment to sharing their faith coincided with the start of a Youth for Christ Campus Life group, which began small and quickly grew to more than 200 students.

Moose was a writer, covering sports for local newspapers and his school paper. He began making plans to attend Moody Bible Institute in Chicago two years later to get a year of Bible training before pursuing a career in newspapering. The follow-ing summer, he returned to Camp Hickory as assistant sports director.

ANOTHER ENCOUNTER

Being there week after week for camps for all ages made 1966 the ultimate summer. Moose heard different speakers on different topics every week and formed strong friendships with the staff. He got in trouble for ordering pencils stamped with: "Camp Hickory, where Christ is 1st and mosquitoes are second." He grew close to Dan and Joyce Ankerberg and their son, Bill, now a California pastor.

One night, while racing around in the dark playing Capture the Flag with other staffers, Moose came upon the director's cabin and noticed the light on and shade open. He crept close and peeked in, only to find Dan and Joyce kneeling on the wood floor in prayer. Even in private, they lived their faith. Concern for souls was at the core of their beings.

Late in the summer, Dan Ankerberg was speaking at teen camp when Moose had yet another encounter with God. Dan explained that while all Christians should be full-time Christians, regardless of their occupations, some are called to full-time Christian work. This time God seemed to sneak up on Moose. Rather than being under conviction, he was simply overwhelmed with the feeling that he should commit himself to full-time Christian work.

When Dan asked for those who felt the call to stand and come forward, Moose went. He thought he was giving up his writing career, probably obligated now to become a pastor or missionary—neither of which he felt drawn to or prepared for. He had to learn that when God calls a person to something, He will equip him and often has already given him a bent in a certain area.

CALLED TO SERVE

Just five years later, when Moose was newly married and working as a sportswriter and photographer for a local newspaper, he caught a glimpse of his reflection in a window. There he was, suit and tie, all grown up, married, and working. And he was reminded of that call. It was time to follow through with it.

He called various Christian organizations, looking for work in writing, editing, and publishing. Moose was hired at Scripture Press where he became editor of a high school Sunday school paper. From there, he went on to become editor of a Christian radio and TV guide, then became managing editor of *Moody* magazine in Chicago. He eventually became publisher at Moody Press and finally vice president for publishing.

In the meantime, on the side, he wrote more than 150 books, including many about professional athletes.

It's been said that big doors turn on small hinges. Moose traces his life's work and ministry back to those two consecutive summers at Camp Hickory where God spoke to him through His servants.

Statistics show that more than a quarter-million become believers at CCI/USA member camps and conferences each year. And more than 500,000 Christian leaders trace their choice of profession to decisions made at camp.

But these are more than statistics. Each represents someone who was once a malleable, impressionable kid who was open to the Spirit on a hot summer night, perhaps unlike he or she had ever been before or would be again. Countless camp works and volunteers never know whom they might be influencing or what might become of the camper or young staff who is listening.

Moose, too, is more than a statistic. I ought to know.

Moose was my nickname.

This article, first published in the September/October 2003 issue of *Christian Camp & Conference Journal,* is used with permission. Copyright 2003 Christian Camp and Conference Association.

RECOMMENDED READING LIST FOR WRITERS

Forgive the shameless plug, but read anything from Writer's Digest Books. I read almost any writing book I can get my hands on, and theirs are consistently the best, most thorough, and helpful.

The watershed Writer's Digest Books title for me was Dean Koontz's *How to Write Best-Selling Fiction* (1981), now out of print. Used copies are gold, available from $70 and up. If you can find one, devour it.

In my opinion, two of the best nonfiction books published in my lifetime are *In Cold Blood* by Truman Capote (Random House, 1965) and *All Over But the Shoutin'* (Vintage, 1997).

Miscellaneous Must-Reads

Advice to Writers, compiled and edited by Jon Winokur (Random House, 1999)

The Best American Sports Writing of the Century by David Halberstam, Editor and Glenn Stout, Series Editor (Houghton Mifflin Company, 1999)

The Best Writing on Writing edited by Jack Heffron (Story Press, 1994)

The Best Writing on Writing, Volume Two edited by Jack Heffron (Story Press, 1995)

Creating Fiction edited by Julie Checkoway (Story Press, 1999)

The Elements of Style by William Strunk Jr and E. B. White (Longman, 2000)

The Fiction Editor, The Novel, and The Novelist by Thomas McCormack (St. Martin's Press, 1988)

For the Love of Books by Ronald B. Schwartz (Penguin Putnam, Inc, 1999)

Gathering and Writing the News by John Paul Jones (Nelson-Hall, 1976)

How to Grow a Novel: The Most Common Mistakes Writers Make and How to Overcome Them by Sol Stein (St. Martin's Griffin, 1999)

An Introduction to Christian Writing by Ethel Herr (Write Now Publications, 2000)

Letters to a Fiction Writer edited by Frederick Busch (W.W. Norton & Company, 1999)

The Little Guide to Your Well-Read Life by Steve Leveen (Levenger Press, 2005)

Native Sons by James Baldwin and Sol Stein (Random House, 2004)

On Writing by Stephen King (Pocket, 2002)

Passion and Craft: Conversations with Notable Writers edited by Bonnie Lyons and Bill Oliver (University of Illinois Press, 1998)

Stein on Writing: A Master Editor of Some of the Most Successful Writers of Our Century Shares His Craft Techniques and Strategies by Sol Stein (St. Martin's Griffin, 2000)

Reality and the Vision edited by Philip Yancey (Word Publishing, 1990)

The Right to Write by Julia Cameron (Penguin Putnam, 1998)

Self-Editing for Fiction Writers by Renni Browne and Dave King (HarperCollins, 1993)

Story by Robert McKee (HarperCollins, 1997)

Techniques of Novel Writing edited by A.S. Burack (The Writer, Inc., 1973)

Why I Write: Thoughts on the Craft of Fiction edited by Will Blythe (Little, Brown & Company, 1998)

Write Away by Elizabeth George (HarperCollins, 2004)

The Writer's Book of Hope by Ralph Keyes (Henry Holt and Company, 2003)

The Writer's Desk by Jill Krementz (Random House, 1996)

Writers on Writing edited by James N. Watkins (Wesleyan Publishing House, 2005)

INDEX

M

MacDonald, John D., 180

magazines, writing for, 74

mannerisms
in attributions, 190–191
of punctuation and type, 191

Manning, Madeline, 158–160

manuscripts
backing up, 135
professional, 18, 200–201, 205–208

margins, 207

Margo mysteries, 132–133, 203, 150,

motivation, characters', 152–153

Motta, Dick, 22–23, 169

Muse, trusting the, 89

music, as inspiration, 60

N

Nack, William, 100–101

networking, 204

New King James Bible, 60

newsletters, writing for, 72

newspapers
as idea source, 77
writing for, 13, 21, 72, 73–74

nonfiction vs. fiction, 41

O

omniscient point of view, 162, 165

On Writing, 128

online research, 117

on-the-nose writing, 187, 190

Operative, The, 153

opportunities, looking for new, 203–204

outlining, 127–128, 135–136

overexplaining, 174–176, 190

P

pace, 125

parables, 41, 137

paragraphs, short, 185

partner, writing, 21

passion
writing about your, 11, 40
in your writing, 57

past tense, 184

Patterson, James, 185

Payton, Walter, 47–53

perfectionistic thinking, dangers of, 59

perspective, 161–168

taking a break from, 90, 91–92

unprofessional, 57

what you know, 4, 11, 72, 75

as work, 8, 35, 194, 200

your best, 35–37, 39–41, 197–198

writing partner, 21

writing space, setting up, 84–86

Y

Youngest Hero, The, 71, 76, 184–185

Your Best Life Now, 213

youth summer camp, 16–17

ABOUT THE AUTHOR

Though much of Jerry Jenkins's life has been spent writing, editing, and publishing in the inspirational market, you don't have to be a person of faith to benefit from this book. Jenkins has enjoyed an unusually diverse career over three-plus decades, even before penning the mega-bestselling Left Behind series of novels—of which seven in a row reached number one on the bestseller lists of the *New York Times*, *USA Today*, the *Wall Street Journal*, and *Publishers Weekly*.

His writing has appeared in *Time, Reader's Digest, Writer's Digest, Parade*, the in-flight magazines of both American Airlines and United Airlines, and dozens of other publications. He was featured on the cover of *Newsweek* magazine in May 2004, when the Left Behind series reached sixty-two million in sales.

Readers familiar only with his Left Behind novels may not realize that Jenkins is the author of more than 155 published books and that his career has also included stints as a sportswriter, photographer, sports editor, magazine editor, magazine publisher, book editor, book publisher, biographer, marriage and family author, syndicated cartoon strip writer (Gil Thorp, 1996–2004), and graduate school writing instructor (Wheaton College, Daystar University, Moody Bible Institute).

Jerry's biographies have included books about Hank Aaron, Walter Payton, Meadowlark Lemon, B.J. Thomas, Orel Hershiser, Nolan Ryan, Mike Singletary, Joe Gibbs, Billy Graham, Bill Gaither, and many others.

Jerry owns the Christian Writers Guild (www.ChristianWritersGuild. com), which partners mentors with writing students via e-mail courses designed for writers aged eight and up to adult, and Jenkins Entertainment (www.Jenkins-Entertainment.com), a Los Angeles–based filmmaking company.

Jenkins has been awarded two honorary doctorates: in humane letters from Bethel College, and in letters from Trinity International University.

Dr. Jenkins and his wife Dianna have three grown sons and three grandchildren, and reside in Colorado.